Your Brain on Pickleball

Using the Psychology of Peak Performance to Raise Your Game to the Next Level

Joseph C. Montgomery, PhD

Copyright © 2025 by Joseph C. Montgomery, PhD

All rights reserved.

Published by As You Wish Publishing

ISBN: 978-1-951131-78-4

Library of Congress Control Number: 2025902402

No portion of this book may be reproduced in any form without written permission from the publisher or author, except as permitted by U.S. copyright law.

Acknowledgements

I was able to complete this book thanks in large part to the support I received on the home front from my fiancé, Sue Waight. She has been very patient with my need to spend lots of time at home writing on the computer or gathering research materials for the various topics in the chapters. It has taken nearly a year to complete the book. Her help really kicked into gear last month when I suffered a mild heart attack and had to have double bypass heart surgery. She spent countless hours with me at the hospital, drove me to doctor appointments, communicated with the doctors for me when needed, organized my medications, and kept a watchful eye over my recovery. I am sorry to say we had to cancel several trips, including a visit to her daughter and family in Maryland and her sister's family in New York. and we had to forego a month in Palm Springs, CA, scheduled for December. She took it all in stride although I know she was disappointed. In short, the book could not have been completed without her help.

I would like to acknowledge the contributions of my former advisor from graduate school at Colorado State University, Jack Hautaluoma, Ph.D. He reviewed each chapter as I completed them, checking for consistency with research findings and relevance of the psychological concepts I was applying. It was a pleasure to renew a working relationship with Jack after a long time apart. I have always been grateful for the support and guidance he provided when I was struggling through graduate school in the early 1980s.

I also acknowledge contributions from Carney Lucas, a 5.0 tournament pickleball player who is an instructor and church pastor with a doctorate in leadership. He reviewed my book chapters for accuracy and relevance, providing valuable feedback and direction. Each time we had a pickleball practice session, he kindly addressed any problems or issues I was experiencing and patiently worked with me on corrective actions. He has always been encouraging of my efforts to improve even at my age; I am 75 years old this year.

I am very grateful to my editor, Candace Devary (Senior Consultant, Devary Communications), who agreed to edit my book chapters. Candace graduated from high school with me in 1967 and we have been friends for many years. I spoke with her at a high school reunion a few months ago and was grateful when she agreed to take on this project. I think the writing quality is much improved thanks to her input.

I received a lot of support from other family members, including my daughters Ketra Isaacson (and her husband Andrew) and Whitney Herric (and her husband Scott). I also appreciate the encouragement of Sue's adult children, Christina Saavedra (and her husband Andrew) and James Hoffski (and his partner Samantha Perez).

Finally, I am grateful for the support and feedback that came from a number of local players who read one or more chapters of my book and encouraged me to continue. Here, I include Steve Wallenfells (5.0 player, instructor at the Pacific Clinic), Mari Willis (local 4.5 player), Damon Little (5.0 player, head of pickleball programs at the Pacific Clinic), Paul

Jones (head of pickleball programs at the Tri-Cities Court Club), Troy Roberts (local 4.5 player), and Phil Sheely (local 4.0 player).

Praise for Your Brain on Pickelball

With a unique blend of cognitive psychology and practical strategies, Your Brain on Pickleball is an insightful guide for players eager to advance their game. Drawing on decades of research and personal experience, the author offers actionable steps to overcome plateaus, build new skills, and harness the power of deliberate practice to elevate performance both on and off the court. **Summer Hess, triathlete/President, Sage Consulting**

While physical skills are important, the right mindset is key to taking your pickleball game to the next level. This book will help you develop mental strategies to stay focused, build confidence, and perform under pressure, giving you the edge on the court. **Paul Jones, Pickleball Director/Columbia Basin Racket Club**

If you want to understand how to improve your pickleball skills and increase your level of play, you really need to read Your Brain on Pickleball. When I was beginning to play and learn pickleball, it was extremely hard to figure out the pickleball rating system and correlating skills. Chapter 4 would have saved me a lot of trial and error. Even now as a higher-level player, this book has helped to identify modifications to my drilling routines and to better understand my partner's play dynamics. Your Brain on Pickleball was an easy conversational read that was entertaining. **Mari Willis, Senior Environmental Specialist, Portland General Power/4.5 pickleball player**

In this book Joe Montgomery shows his love of pickleball and shares an important value- he thinks we should try to be as good as we can be in doing the things we love. Life is a gift, and we should use it as well as we can. He includes current research and theory from psychology to show how this can be done for pickleball. If you like pickleball-even a little-you should read this book. **Jack Hautaluoma, Ph.D., Professor of Psychology, Colorado State University (retired)**

As a long-time competitive athlete and elite coach, I am always looking for resources that address the complexities of improving performance. If you're new to pickleball or competing in national tournaments- Joe Montgomery's well-organized and approachable style addresses everything you need to know to take your physical and mental game to the next level. **Steve Wallenfells, novelist and freelance writer with 40+ years as a competitive athlete and coach**

Contents

Foreword   XV

1. Why So Few Pickleball Players Move Up to the Next Level   1
   Strategy #1: Practice regularly, with intensity
   Strategy # 2: Obtain feedback and track performance
   Strategy # 3: Identify and adopt the shots and skills needed for the next level
   Strategy # 4: Maintain sufficient focus, concentration, and awareness
   Strategy # 5: Overcome limiting beliefs

2. Improving Pickleball Skills Through Practice   13
   Practice from the perspective of brain functioning
   System 1 and System 2 Thinking
   Neuroplasticity
   Cognitive biases and heuristics
   What peak performance literature tells us about practice
   Summary and Conclusions
   Life Lesson

3. Feedback and Tracking   35
   Psychological biases that make us resistant to feedback
   Feedback from practice sessions
   Feedback from backboard practice sessions

    Feedback from coaches and observers
    Video recording your drilling sessions and games
    Using a charting tool to quantify and track your performance
    Learn from Failure
    Life Lesson

4. The Skills You Need for the Next Level   59
    Why you may not know what's needed at the next level
    Identifying what you need for the next level
    A summary of characteristics for each level
    Characteristics of 2.5-level players
    Characteristics of 3.0-level players
    Characteristics of 3.5-level players
    Characteristics of 4.0-level players
    Characteristics of 4.5-level players
    Characteristics of 5.0-level level players
    Characteristics of 5.5+ level players
    Using the Pareto principle to help identify key areas for improvement
    Life Lesson

5. Improving Focus and Concentration   77
    The cognitive demands of pickleball
    Consequences of poor concentration
    Why it's hard to maintain concentration and focus
    The impacts of Default Mode Network thinking
    Exercises to stay more in a Task Positive Mode, less in a Default Mode
    Using mindfulness meditation

Practicing Task Positive Network / Mindfulness between points
Incorporating Task Positive Mode / Mindfulness into your game
Improving sensory awareness and focus
Awareness and focus of attention
Attitudes while using mindfulness
Deepening our focus and concentration while playing
Concentration exercises
Exercise 1: Holding an image
Exercise 2: Manipulating images
Exercise 3: Attention to detail
Exercise 4: Pushing the limits of your attention span
Exercise 5: Impulse control
Life Lesson

6. How Limiting Beliefs Affect our Performance   103
    Beliefs as a survival mechanism
    How beliefs affect thoughts, feelings, and actions
    The Positive Belief Pathway
    The Limiting Belief Pathway
    More on the Positive Belief Pathway
    The evidence relative to beliefs and athletic performance
    The origin of limiting beliefs
    A closer look at limiting versus empowering beliefs
    The role of the Default Mode Network in maintaining limiting beliefs
    Applying life lessons

7. Reprogramming Limiting Beliefs   123

Approach 1: David Bayer's method for reprogramming limiting beliefs

The process for changing limiting beliefs

Become aware of the limiting belief.

Make a new decision.

Find evidence that the new decision is true.

Realizing the benefits of the Broaden and Build pathway

The brain as a search engine

Approach 2: Carol Dweck's Fixed versus Growth Mindset approach

The problematic aspects of a fixed mindset

The benefits of a Growth Mindset

Applying the Fixed verses Growth Mindset approach to pickleball

Approach 3: Reprogramming negative beliefs using self-talk

The self-talk reprogramming process

Using self-talk and visualization to improve skills

Approach 4: Reprogramming limiting beliefs by disputing their logic

Using logic to counter false, irrational, and negative thoughts

Identifying and correcting limiting beliefs

Chapter Summary

Life Lesson

8. Putting It All Together 155

Strategy 1: Practice regularly with intensity

Strategy 2: Obtain feedback and track performance

Strategy 3: Identify and adopt shots and skills needed for the next level

Strategy 4: Maintain sufficient focus, concentration, and awareness

Strategy 5: Overcome limiting beliefs

Transforming limiting beliefs into empowering beliefs

Reengineering negative beliefs

Changing from a Fixed to a Growth Mindset

Repetition of verbal statements

Identifying the logical flaws of your limiting beliefs

Next Steps   169

References   173

Appendix   179

   Appendix A: Pickleball Game Charting Tool

   Appendix B: Comparisons of Pickleball Skills with the Next Level

Foreword

By Carney Lucas 5.0 player/instructor/pastor

When I first found Pickleball, I fell in love. Like many others, I was hooked the second I held a wooden paddle in my hand. Not only did I want to play as much as I possibly could, I also wanted to get better as fast as I could. I consumed content, teachings, clinics, and camps. I spent hours and hours scouring forums, YouTube, and other sites searching for tips, tricks, and silver bullets to level up my game.

I imagine you may have a similar goal, evidenced by the fact that you're holding this book in your hands right now. Growth and progression in our pickleball game is often a desire for everyone who steps foot on a court and discovers the passion that pickleball offers.

While there are so many physical tips and training resources out there, a large opportunity for growth is not talked about much. The physical, connected with the mental and psychological aspect of sports, has yet to truly enter into the pickleball space.

As someone who works with professional athletes in Major League Baseball, I am often struck by the small differences of the ones who make it, juxtaposed with the many who do not. Nearly every account as to why one makes it and another doesn't has nothing to do with physical talent and abilities. Rather, it's nearly always mental, emotional, and psychological maturity that determines a professional baseball player's trajectory and future success.

Pickleball is no different. To reach our fullest potential on the pickleball court, we must grow in the physical, as well as the psychological and mental parts of the game. Joe's book offers a way. I hope that Joe's offerings can help, challenge, grow, and unlock new ideas for you in your pickleball game development.

Chapter One

Why So Few Pickleball Players Move Up to the Next Level

If you are trying to move to the next level in pickleball, as I am, you know how hard it is. I began playing pickleball in 2017 at the 3.0 level, and I gradually worked up through the 3.5 and 4.0 levels. Now, I am playing at the 4.5 level for the 50+ age group. I think my tennis background accelerated the process quite a bit. I played tennis on the University of Washington tennis team in the early '70s, and I continued to play tournament level tennis for about 40 years before arthritis in my knees compelled me to give it up. Nonetheless, it has taken quite a bit of time and a lot of effort (including a lot of fun!) to progress to each higher level.

I am a 75-year-old research-oriented psychologist with a Ph.D. in Industrial/Organizational Psychology (quasi-retired). In my career, I have focused on performance improvement and performance measurement for groups and individuals. I have long studied the research on "peak performance" and how it is that experts achieve their high levels of performance. Likewise, I have wondered why so many performers fail to perform at an expert level. I have found considerable literature on both peak and mediocre performance, and I will summarize much of it and its applications to pickleball in this book. My research has been of increasing interest to me personally as I have grown older and work to stay competitive with younger players.

In my observations of pickleball players over the past seven years, I have found that many have improved certain aspects of their game over time, but very few players have actually moved up to a higher level of play. The exceptions include a few young, talented players with a background in a racket or paddle sport who were discovered early by higher-level players and were carefully mentored through progressive levels of play. These fortunate individuals demonstrated that they could move from a novice level to playing at the 4.5+ level within six months to a year. A few players, aged 50+, myself included, have moved up one or more levels, but we seem to be in the minority.

Most of the players I have seen or played with over the past five years are still basically playing at the same level. Most of the 3.0 level players remain at the 3.0 level, "3.5s" remain at the 3.5 level, and so forth. I have certainly seen gradual improvement in these players in terms of their basic shot-making. Some of the 3.5s have become really strong 3.5s! I have tried to find research about the percentage of pickleball players who move up a level and how long that takes, but it appears no one really knows. It is estimated that around 70% of pickleball players are relatively new to the sport and are at or below the 3.0 level of play (Carvana PPA Tour Website, 2024). Around 20 to 30% of players are in the 3.0 to 4.0 skill level, leaving about 10% of players at the 4.0+ levels. The rapid growth of the sport (158% in the past three years) suggests there is an increasing number of players at the beginning levels (Gilman, 2023,

Carvana PPA Tour Website). Around 20% of those players are in the 55+ age group and they may not move up as quicky as younger players., However, there are no data on that issue, and I prefer to believe this is not true! I have even run several artificial intelligence (AI) searches on the topic, for example, using *Perplexity AI*, which is an AI-Powered search engine and chatbot that answers user queries. *Perplexity* estimated that 10 to 20% of pickleball players move on to the next level, but the site provided no data to support this "opinion."

There is plenty of research on moving from a novice to an expert level of performance in other areas. Malcolm Gladwell (2016) popularized the research finding that it takes about 10,000 hours of practice for a novice to become an expert at nearly anything. This is good news, because it disproves the idea that some people are just naturally more talented than others. Basically, we can improve at anything if we put in the time and effort. The bad news is that the practice must be intense, pushing us past the edge of our comfort zones. Fortunately, however, we don't need 10,000 hours of practice (about 10 years) to progress, e.g., from a 3.5 to a 4.0 level. As you might expect, however, significant learning time is required.

One of the themes of this book is that becoming really good at one level is a necessary, but not a sufficient, condition for playing at the next level! Playing at a higher level requires additional shots, new strategies, and a higher level of physical strength and conditioning. For example, in order for 3.5-level players to play at the 4.0 level or higher, they need to add a good third shot drop and a strong dinking game (as well as other shots). They need to develop greater consistency and use new strategies. Unfortunately, I don't see many 3.5-level players systematically working to improve these skills and strategies. It requires regular practice or drilling sessions and very few players like to drill or practice, for reasons that will be discussed shortly. In my experience, very few 4.0-level players have a good third shot drop or effective dinks, and I don't see many of them working on those shots. Again, in my experience, very few 4.0-level players drill or practice regularly or at all. I have been mystified by the unwillingness of many players to learn the shots and strategies needed to move up.

I finally concluded that the reason players aren't moving up is that they play too much and practice too little. The next chapter discusses, from a psychological point of view, why people are resistant to practice and just want to play the game. (It also provides a framework for the most effective types of practice.) In researching this book, I came across a number of writers, in a variety of sports and performance areas, who assert that performance often stagnates and/or declines when players do not incorporate time for learning, experimentation, and practice.

Eduardo Briceno in *The Performance Paradox* (2023) devotes an entire book to describing how performance without a practice component leads, paradoxically, to reduced performance. Without learning and practicing, skills plateau and performance becomes stale and repetitive. He gives many examples in sports, as well as business, hobbies, and even cooking. For example, in chess, players who spend the most time competing in tournaments are not those who reach the highest ranks. In medicine, the more physicians practice medicine, the worse their patient outcomes (Khullar, 2023). Many of us spend hours typing away at our computers but we don't become world-class typists. Richard Williams was well aware of the performance paradox issue when he began teaching Venus and Serena to play tennis. He kept them out of tournaments when they were young, devoting all their time to practice rather than matches. (His strategy for getting his daughters to the top through intense practice is documented in the biographical movie *King Richard*.)

Sometime after I concluded pickleball players weren't advancing because they played too much, as I was reviewing some recent findings about brain functioning, I had an epiphany. These findings provided valuable insights into why pickleball players end up stuck at a certain level and fail to improve their performance! At that ah-ha moment, I decided to write this book relating brain functioning to pickleball. It was an opportunity to apply several of my favorite hobbies and interests (cognitive psychology, pickleball, and expert performance) in an enjoyable writing project! In actuality, it wasn't as easy to research and write as I initially anticipated, but it has been amazingly gratifying. Now, nearly a year later, here we are!

In this book I will discuss several aspects of the way our brains function that make it quite challenging to engage in the behaviors needed to improve at pickleball. First, I want to point out that the human brain developed or evolved from very ancient times to help us survive in a very hostile and dangerous environment. Humans were designed for survival, not to be good pickleball players, sad to say! In fact, the brain's design for survival in a hostile environment actually makes our brains ill-adapted for survival in a modern, high-tech, and physically safe world (Kahneman, 2011). For example, the brain's inherent focus on being alert to danger distracts us from being productive and creative. It predisposes us to feelings of anxiety and stress (Grant, 2021).

In addition to being hardwired for survival, there are other aspects of brain functioning that can explain why it is difficult to learn new pickleball skills and strategies. For example, cognitive psychologist Daniel Kahneman (2006) created a model of a "System 1" automatic thinking part of the brain and a "System 2" conscious thinking part. System 1 has enormous storage capacity and acts with lightning speed. It contrasts with the "System 2" conscious part of the brain which has very limited storage and information processing capacity. We can only keep a few things in our mind at one time. System 2 also has very limited energy supplies and conserves them whenever possible. This translates to being mentally lazy in many situations (e.g., "I don't want to practice my third shot drop"). Further, due to its information processing shortcomings, System 2 is subject to a number of "cognitive biases" and heuristics (shortcuts in thinking) that make the brain function less than rationally in many situations. I will show how these aspects of brain functioning affect our ability to play higher-level pickleball.

With the basics of cognitive functioning in mind, I developed a set of five strategies for overcoming the difficulties of improving pickleball skills and moving quickly and efficiently to playing at the next level. As discussed below and more fully in subsequent chapters, the strategies include:

1. Strategy #1: Practice regularly, with intensity

2. Strategy # 2: Obtain feedback and track performance

3. Strategy # 3: Identify and adopt the shots and skills needed for the next level

4. Strategy # 4: Maintain sufficient focus, concentration, and awareness

5. Strategy # 5: Overcome limiting beliefs.

Strategy #1: Practice regularly, with intensity

Most people enjoy playing so much they are not willing to "lose" valuable playing time with practice sessions (an example of the "Loss Aversion" bias). As a result, most players simply do not practice enough to improve. Unfortunately, considerable research has shown that skill improvement is highly dependent on focused practice (Ericsson, 2016, Kahneman, 2011, Sayed, 2010).

Whereas recreational players rarely practice, professional players practice a lot! In fact, many pros spend at least twice as much time practicing as they do playing (Derickson, 2023; Johns 2023). For recreational players who don't practice, their brain's System 2 component may not want to expend the necessary energy needed to improve. Furthermore, they don't want to give up the immediate gratification of playing for the delayed gratification of long-term improvement (yet another cognitive bias). Even when they do practice, they tend to work only on aspects of the game that they have already mastered, and they avoid the "hard work" of tackling their weaknesses (another bias at work here, as well). In Chapter 2, I focus on the most effective ways to structure practice sessions for improvement that can help you move to the next level of play.

Strategy # 2: Obtain feedback and track performance

Feedback, especially immediate and accurate feedback, complements practice as a key element in any learning situation (Juncewicz, 2017;

Kahneman, 2011; Sayed, 2010). Unfortunately, competitive games of pickleball provide very little useful feedback. The points are over quickly and the next point begins immediately, leaving no time for reflection. There is such a variety of possible shots that there is little likelihood of immediately repeating a shot to correct an earlier mistake. Consequently, we have to rely on practice and drilling, feedback from coaches and mentors, and even making video recordings of our game performance to get good feedback. Furthermore, due to a number of cognitive biases and mental shortcomings, we rarely ask for feedback from others about what could be done to improve; and, in fact, we actively resist such feedback. Chapter 3 provides recommendations for getting more feedback, a process for video recording and charting games, and information for computing a variety of performance-related statistics.

Strategy # 3: Identify and adopt the shots and skills needed for the next level

The basic issue underlying this strategy is that often we <u>don't know</u> what new skills and strategies are needed to play well at the next level. Many players believe that continuing to improve their current skills will somehow move them up to the next level. However, this is simply not true. The next higher level involves new shots, skills, and strategies; but few players know what higher-level skills are required. This is due to our tendency to rely on System 1 unconscious thinking and for the System 2 conscious awareness to discourage us from devoting sufficient energy to challenging the status quo. There are several additional cognitive biases that make us unaware of the higher-level skills and unreceptive to the effort required to achieve them. Chapter 4 lays out an approach for you to identify the new shots and strategies needed to move up to the next level, regardless of your current level of play.

Strategy # 4: Maintain sufficient focus, concentration, and awareness

Many aspects of the pickleball game require a high level of cognitive performance. The game involves strategic thinking, focus and concentration, mental agility, emotional control, spatial awareness, and problem-solving. However, many players are not sufficiently focused and make repeated unforced errors, often without even realizing it. Staying focused requires maintaining a state of awareness and mindfulness, both during and between points. Chapter 5 provides a number of strategies and exercises for maintaining the high level of mental focus needed for pickleball.

Strategy # 5: Overcome limiting beliefs

Many of us believe we are too old, too fat, too slow, too uncoordinated, etc. to play at the next level. Many of us struggle with feelings of low self-worth, believing that we aren't "good enough" to succeed. With these kinds of limiting beliefs, consciously or unconsciously held, there is no way we can perform at our best! The negative thoughts and emotions associated with these beliefs are too disruptive to our performance. These limiting beliefs, which arose from early childhood learning experiences, are not true now, but they continue to haunt us even as adults. Chapters 6 and 7 provide insights on limiting beliefs, their impediments to playing at a higher level, and how to overcome them.

Chapter 6 discusses the impacts of limiting beliefs on performance and how limiting beliefs arise from early childhood experiences. I provide examples of more empowering beliefs that will enhance performance. The chapter contrasts the adverse effects of negative beliefs with the positive effects of empowering beliefs, and it explains how positive emotions create powerful mental and physiological changes that can greatly enhance our capabilities.

Chapter 7 provides four approaches for identifying and reprogramming limiting beliefs. One approach involves tracking back from negative feelings to negative thoughts, to underlying negative beliefs, and then re-engineering these beliefs into more positive and realistic ones. The second approach involves directly reprogramming beliefs through repetition of verbal statements with visualization. The third approach, where we have beliefs that our abilities are "fixed" by genetics or the environment, involves shifting to a "Growth Mindset." The fourth approach involves identifying the irrational or illogical elements of our limiting beliefs and reframing them as more rational and realistic ones.

I am convinced that incorporating these strategies into your pickleball improvement efforts will pay huge and immediate dividends in your pickleball play! You don't have to use all the strategies at the same time, just gradually add bits and pieces of them into your practice and improvement efforts. I hope you enjoy the next chapters as I describe the strategies and their relationship to various aspects of brain functioning. Although the information is directed primarily at pickleball, I have included a "Life Lesson" section at the end of each chapter, which explains how the strategies can be applied beneficially to other areas of your life.

I maintain that the general failure of pickleball players to incorporate these strategies in their improvement efforts explains why so few players advance to the next level. In the following chapters, I will discuss the strategies in more depth, link them to peculiarities of our cognitive functioning, and provide step-by-step approaches for implementing them in our pickleball play and more broadly in our lives. The discussion will draw on research from the fields of learning theory, cognitive psychology, neuroplasticity, and personality psychology as well as the expert performance literature to develop these strategies.

Chapter Two

Improving Pickleball Skills Through Practice

Most pickleball players would much rather spend their time playing than practicing. They aren't willing to "lose" valuable playing time to practice sessions. They prefer the immediate gratification of playing to the delayed gratification of performance improvements they can achieve through practice. Sad to say, our brains are hardwired more for instant gratification than for long-term gratification! A game situation is generally a lot easier, more fun, and more immediately rewarding than practice. Points in a game are fairly short, they end, and there is a pause before the next point to catch your breath. At the end of a game, there is a tangible result, a win or a loss. Practice sessions, on the other hand, are physically demanding and require considerable mental focus. They can seem methodical and tedious. Ultimately, however, they produce results, i.e., skills improvement; but in the short term it can be a frustrating process with delayed benefits.

Bottom line, players can find many reasons NOT to practice, thus, most recreational players simply do not practice. It's understandable and not an issue unless you are trying to move up to the next level, which YOU

ARE! In this chapter I will demonstrate that practice actually can be fun and very rewarding in terms of the pleasure we experience from improved pickleball skills and better play.

As mentioned in the previous chapter, I had noticed that relatively few players were moving to higher levels of play, even after several years of playing the game. I found that troubling and puzzling. I finally concluded that my fellow pickleball players play too much and practice too little. I'm not alone in this opinion. I have come across a number of writers, in a variety of sports and performance areas, who believe that just playing games or performing without incorporating time for learning, experimentation, and practice leads to stagnation and even a decline in performance.

In Chapter 1, I mentioned Eduardo Briceno's book The Performance Paradox (2023), in which the theme is that performance without practice or a learning component leads, paradoxically, to reduced performance. Briceno maintains that without learning and practicing, our skills plateau and our performance becomes stale and repetitive. He points out that chess players who spend the most time playing in tournaments are not the competition winners who reach the highest ranks. He notes that Richard Williams had the performance paradox in mind when he began teaching his daughters, Venus and Serena Williams, to play tennis. Instead of having them play in matches and compete in tournaments when they were young, he had them devote their time to practice. I remember that when Venus and Serena first appeared in professional tournaments, they were great players, but their tournament competitions were infrequent. I couldn't understand why Richard kept his daughters from playing in all of the tournaments. Now I understand; he knew that too much tournament play would lead to stagnation and burnout. His plan was to have them learn and grow so they could play at their maximum ability, hence more practice and less competition. His strategy is quite a contrast to what I see with many pickleball players who play for hours every day of the week without getting any better. In fact, many players seem to get worse as they accumulate various muscle and joint injuries associated with overuse.

Practice from the perspective of brain functioning

The principles of effective practicing that I offer in this chapter are derived directly from an understanding of brain functioning. There are three topics of brain functioning that are of particular interest:

1. System 1 thinking (i.e., fast, unconscious thinking with vast capacity) versus System 2 thinking (i.e., slow, conscious, energy-conserving thinking with very limited capacity),

2. Neuroplasticity and the ability of the brain to grow new neuronal connections and expand the areas of the brain associated with a specific activity

3. Cognitive errors and biases essentially hard-wired into our brains through the process of evolutionary development.

Applying these principles to improvement activities can help players efficiently move their performance to the next level.

System 1 and System 2 Thinking

The concepts of System 1 and System 2 thinking are very important in understanding how we learn to play pickleball. Learning a new pickleball skill initially involves System 2 learning, which includes reading, listening to instruction, and observation. System 2 learning is very slow and inefficient. Our brains may quickly feel overwhelmed or exhausted if we try to take in too much information at one time. System 2 is the analytical mode of thinking; it requires conscious effort and attention. It is the thinking mode involved in complex activities such as performing calculations, solving problems, and making informed decisions.

Once we have a conscious understanding of the new skill, we must rehearse and practice it for some time before it becomes a more automatic System 1 activity or habit. Thus, the focus begins with System 2 conscious learning, which gradually declines as the skill becomes more automatic and habitual with System 1 automatic thinking. System 1 is the dominant mode of thinking. It generates most of our thoughts and behaviors automatically. Dittmar (2024) estimates that about 95% of our daily thoughts and activities are based on habits.

The two systems work together smoothly and efficiently in most situations. Each system has some shortcomings, however. System 1 can unconsciously adopt errors in perception and judgment that may not be noticed by System 2. For example, System 1 may hold unconscious, negative beliefs about our abilities, dating back to early childhood experiences. These biases and beliefs can be very difficult to modify as long as they remain unconscious.

System 2 limitations on information processing mean that we are easily overwhelmed with information and need to focus on one or two skills at a time. Furthermore, System 2 expends significant energy when it functions and, applying a sort of energy conservation strategy, the brain tends to limit System 2 actions whenever possible. As a result, System 2 is inclined to be lazy (that is, energy-conserving) and willing to take shortcuts to avoid using a lot of energy. This is a partial explanation of why practice is not very appealing to many players.

Consider how we use System 2 thinking when starting to learn a new pickleball skill or strategy. In learning to dink, for example, we start by learning the principles for hitting the shot (bend your knees, lift upwards with the paddle, aim higher than the net, etc.). We practice these rules consciously, mentally saying them to ourselves as we try to hit dinks on the court. Usually, our first attempts aren't very successful, and we have to keep adjusting our stroke, footwork, balance etc. until the dink starts going in consistently. As we become more skilled with the basics (System 1 learning), we can add more complexity, returning to System 2 for new information uptake. Eventually, we hit the dink successfully and with much less effort and thought. We are then ready to move on to a different skill, which we build up through System 2 learning and gradually integrate it into our play with our other skills via System 1.

What are the implications of applying this process for the best skills improvement strategies? First, much of our practice time should be spent on System 2, conscious learning, i.e., focusing on learning and upgrading a single new skill or a few skills. Practicing skills that are mostly at the System 1 level (e.g., shots that you already know how to hit) provides little value because you already have these skills. It is an inefficient use of your time. *Instead, your practice sessions should focus on developing new skills in which you don't have a sufficient level of comfort or proficiency.*

Second, playing recreational, competitive games is not the best way to improve. Game play doesn't let you focus on one or two particular skill-building areas (instead, you are working on everything at once), so you can't engage in repetition of a particular stroke to improve your performance. In addition, during games there is no opportunity to get feedback about your shots, which can be useful for improvement. Games proceed rapidly, points go by quickly, the game is over, and you have no clear idea of what was working and what was not. In short, playing games is a very ineffective way to develop new skills. This might seem counterintuitive, but it is consistent with how learning occurs. Playing games will certainly complement your practice activities and help integrate new skills into your game repertoire, however, it is quite limiting by itself. It is no wonder that some people can play every day for years and make only minimal improvements in their skills! They are not advancing their player skills; they are merely rehearsing System 1 automatic behaviors.

Third, the way our brains learn new skills has to do with intensity of practice. Ericsson (2010) and others have shown that practice needs to be performed at an intense level for maximum learning to take place. The level of intensity needed for rapid learning is one where we feel challenged to perform the action properly. It is not just hitting 100 forehands in a rote, automatic fashion. It is engaging in challenging practice that requires mental acuity. physical coordination, and exertion. It can be a lot of fun and very rewarding! With practice, you can learn a new skill very quickly and put it to use in your game in a short time. Your System 2 brain, however, is likely to experience some resistance to expending so much energy and to feeling a bit out of control. You need to overcome this System 2 bias by being acutely aware of System 2's lazy (energy conserving) attitude! The pros overcome this resistance out of a necessity to improve quickly and perform at maximum capacity. It's a reliable approach to meeting their performance goals.

Building on the concepts of System 1 and System 2 brain functioning, we need to allocate regular time for practice and then practice with intensity. We need to continuously introduce new skills and avoid spending too much time on what we already know. As will be discussed further, we also need to practice the most difficult new skills early in the practice session.

Neuroplasticity

Neuroplasticity refers to the brain's ability to be changed and shaped by our actions and the environment (Kwik, 2020). Every time we learn something, new neuronal connections and pathways are made within the brain. If we work to develop a new skill, not only will new pathways be formed in the brain, but the area of the brain dedicated to the skill can increase in size. Research on London cab drivers, famous for memorizing the complex streets of London, has shown that the memory areas of their brains have significantly expanded to hold this extensive information. Every high-level performer in any sport or skill-related activity has vastly expanded neuronal connections associated with these skills and has greater areas in their brains dedicated to performing these skills. Consider that people who have lost their eyesight and try to learn Braille are initially not able to read the Braille dots, primarily because our fingers lack sufficient sensitivity for this task. However, over time and with much practice, the increased neuronal connections and expanded brain regions associated with touch increase finger sensitivity so that people can gradually become capable of reading Braille (Sodato, 1998).

The takeaway for us as pickleball players is that, as we improve our skills through practice, our brains are developing new neuronal connections and there is an expansion of the area in our brains devoted to these skills and motor abilities. *That means our abilities are not fixed, they expand with use!* We become more capable as we practice. Furthermore, our reaction times speed up as well. This increase is facilitated by a process of myelination of the nervous pathways, in which the pathways become coated with a myelin (glial cell) sheath that greatly speeds up transmission of the signal. Practice increases our capacity for high-level performance!

Building the neuronal pathways associated with a new pickleball shot or skill is like building a new highway. You can use the pick and shovel approach. That is, when you hit that shot sporadically during a game, only a few neurons are recruited to the learning task and only a weak electrical signal triggers them. It takes a long time to create the pathway! Alternatively, you can bring in earthmovers, bulldozers and other heavy equipment to build the highway in a hurry. With this intense practice approach, you recruit a large number of neurons, send a very intense electrical signal through them, and build the neural pathway with amazing speed.

Cognitive biases and heuristics

A third area of brain functioning that is relevant to us as pickleball players arises from certain cognitive biases and heuristics (thinking shortcuts) that we all possess. The human brain developed in prehistoric times where the goal was survival in a dangerous environment, not effective performance in the modern world. As a result, some decisions, actions, and perceptions that are natural to us, and are more or less hard-wired to help ensure our survival, are counter-productive in modern society. Three examples of biases that are relevant to pickleball skills include: 1) the Negativity Bias, 2) Loss Aversion, and 3) (I'm not kidding here) "What you see is all there is" (WYSIATI).

Negativity bias arises from how heightened awareness of potential danger helped our ancestors sense danger and respond quickly when needed. People who didn't anticipate danger didn't survive for very long! Today, that same heightened anticipation of danger leads to a "negativity bias" in which we naturally focus on the negative or potentially dangerous aspects of our environment. This negative orientation can make us feel that common situations, e.g., public speaking or a competitive tournament, are unsafe and can trigger the "Fight / Flight / Freeze" syndrome, with high levels of anxiety and stress. The negativity bias also means that we focus on bad things that happen and pay less attention to good things. Thus, in our pickleball game we tend to remember and even exaggerate our mistakes while undervaluing and under-appreciating the positive aspects of our game. We may be overly aware of our weaknesses and relatively unaware of our strengths and skills. Practice can help us overcome a negativity bias by giving us confidence in the reliability of our shots and bypassing the need to think about our shots via System 1 automatic actions. Furthermore, building a competitive aspect to our practice sessions (to be discussed shortly) acclimates us to competition and greatly reduces the stress we experience.

Loss aversion bias arises from the historic need to safeguard our loved ones and food supply. With this cognitive bias, we are much more motivated to avoid losing something than we are to gaining something of similar value. For example, research has shown that the pain of losing $100 is much greater than the pleasure of gaining $100! Loss aversion can make us feel painfully distraught to lose a rally or game, while we may feel only moderate joy from winning a rally or game. Fear of losing can make it difficult to enjoy playing in tournaments and may inhibit trying out new strokes and strategies. When we are learning a new skill, our performance always drops off a bit at first, so it takes some courage to continue trying out the new shot when we are losing points as a result.

I believe this is a huge factor in explaining why so few 3.5 or 4.0-level players learn to hit the third shot drop! Initially they either miss it or it gets smashed by their opponents. Loss aversion keeps us in our comfort zone, unable to try out our new shots in a game environment. It is a powerful force for conservatism and stagnation in our games. Dittmar (2024) believes that not wanting to practice is in itself an example of loss aversion. We perceive that we lose valuable playing time if we choose to practice instead; and the loss of playing time outweighs the gains of skill improvement provided by practice.

A third cognitive bias is known is "What you see is all there is" (WYSIATI), coined by Daniel Kahneman (2016). Its relevance in pickleball is apparent when players at any given level use a limited range of shots and tactics at their level of play and believe that these shots and tactics represent the entire range of pickleball skills. The shots they see are all there is. Another way of saying this is "we don't know what we don't know." Thus, we might think that what is needed to move up to a higher level is just to hit our current shots better, or harder. Nothing could be further from the truth! The relevance of this bias to our practice sessions is that, while we need to be incorporating new shots and tactics in our practice to progress to the next level, we may instead be completely focused on our current skills. We may have no idea about the requirements of the next level of play! Our WYSIATI bias can block our upward progression! Here is where it is helpful to have a coach or a friend who plays at a higher level to help us plan the content of our practice sessions. In a later chapter I address this issue directly by providing a system for identifying next-level skills and techniques to include in your current practice sessions.

What peak performance literature tells us about practice

Research literature on peak performance is entirely consistent with the brain research discussed in the previous section. I will briefly summarize some of the main findings about peak performance in this section.

The role of deliberate practice

Three researchers who studied individual performance offer enlightened observations that are helpful in understanding the influence of brain functioning on productive practicing.

- Ericsson (2010) studied the top performers in a variety of fields, e.g., music, sports, and chess. He found that these experts practiced for significantly more time <u>and</u> with greater intensity than did lower-level performers. He used the term "deliberate practice" to describe the high-intensity practice needed to reach top levels of performance. He found that it takes about 10,000 hours of intense practice to move from novice to expert at nearly any performance activity, which usually amounts to 10 years or so. Yikes! That's a long time. Fortunately, moving up a level of play in pickleball can take a lot less time. Ericsson also noted that when most people practice, they focus on the things that they can do most effortlessly (i.e., they prefer System 1 activities), while experts focus on the most difficult aspects. His view of practice is that every minute you should be trying to extend your mind and body, pushing yourself beyond your current limits. You should be so engaged in the practice that, by the end of the session, you are literally a different person.

- Sayid (2010) drew similar conclusions based on his study of table tennis players. He was a promising but not highly ranked player early in his career. Fortunately, he was able to hire a top Chinese player (who had recently immigrated to Britain) as a coach. At the time, Chinese players were dominating world table tennis, attributed by many Westerners, incorrectly, to genetic factors such as hand speed or reaction times. The new coach showed Sayid that he was suffering from a severe case of WYSIATI. (OK, Sayid did not use that term.) Instead of a conventional practice session, the Chinese coach brought in a bucket of 100 balls and hit them to Sayid in rapid-fire fashion at different angles, speeds, spins, etc., always pushing Sayid to the limits of his speed, movement, technique, anticipation, timing, and agility. As Sayid improved his performance under this intense training, his coach sped up the sessions and increased the difficulty level by extending the width of the table by 50%, which forced Sayid to cover more territory and angles. As you might imagine, Sayid was shocked by the new coach's approach! However, Sayid's tournament performance and world ranking rapidly skyrocketed to new levels. Sayid eventually studied the performance of top athletes engaged in a number of sports and found that intense and extended practice sessions were the common elements of everyone in this group, but not those below the top ranks. Training intensity and duration separated the great from the mediocre. He noted that philosophy of intense and extended practice is common in many sports. It describes the approach Richard Williams used to train his daughters Venus and Serena to become top-level tennis players (Sayid, 2010)!

- Colvin (2015) studied the role of practice in elite versus second-tier figure skaters. He found that elite skaters regularly attempted jumps and moves that were very difficult, even for elite skaters. The elite skaters fell on the ice significantly more frequently than did the lower-level skaters, and they suffered high rates of bruising and injuries as a result, while on their way to elite performance. In contrast, skaters below the elite level often failed to push past their limits, they did not fall nor experience injuries very often (preferring easier moves they practiced), and, as a result, they did not improve their performance levels. Like the other researchers, Colvin concluded that elite performers had no innate ability or talent advantage. Rather, achieving elite performance was the result of their approach to practice. For those of us who want to move up a level or even further in pickleball, having some rare level of innate ability is not a consideration! We just need to practice.

Practicing the most difficult skills early in practice

Another important research finding is that the most challenging drills need to be done up front. Many of us practice what we are familiar with first and save the hard drills until last (again, a System 2s preference). Doing the easiest aspects first means we spend most of the time on the easy parts, leaving very little time for pushing into new territory with our skills. Not only do we spend little time on the more difficult skills, but we are also usually too tired at the end of a practice session to apply the intensity required to make the difficult drills productive. Laido Dittmar (2024) has nicely captured this idea in graphic form. Figure 1 shows practice difficulty over time for two different approaches. The diagonal line indicates the level of energy remaining for us during the practice session. The easy-first approach adds difficulty at the end of the practice session, leading to less intensity of effort when working on the most difficult shots or skills because our energy levels are low at that point. This results in relatively slow progress in spite of practicing. The hard-first approach involves practicing the most difficult aspects early on, right after warmup, so that you can work on those aspects when you are fresh and energetic. With this approach, the result is effective progress over time.

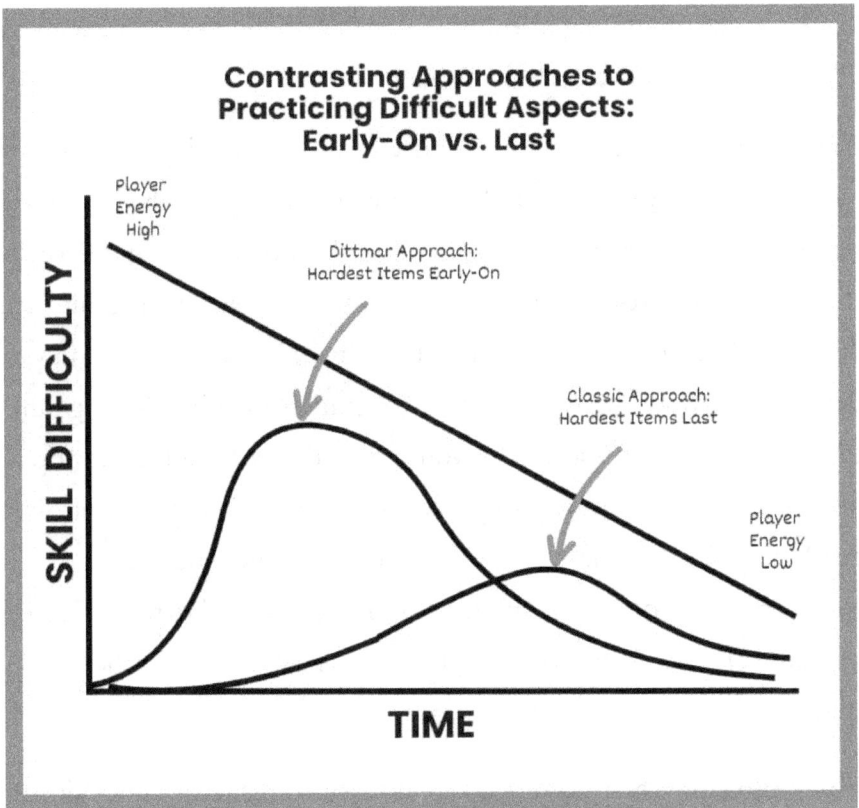

Figure 1. Practicing difficult skills early versus late in drill sessions (Laido Dittmar (2024)

Using progressions in practice sessions

Effective practice also requires that we continue to increase the difficulty levels of each drill as our skill improves. People often experience rapid progress initially in developing a new skill, then improvement slows down and eventually seems to stop. Progress seems to slow down because of an inherent "adaptation effect." Initially, practicing a new shot requires full concentration and effort. Over time, less focus and effort are required as the new skill becomes more automatic (System 1). Just as in weightlifting, where we have to keep increasing the weight lifted to increase strength, the difficulty of each drill has to be gradually increased in order to keep improving.

Applied to pickleball practice, we need to move quickly from low to high difficulty levels. To coach a beginner working on the dink shot, we might start by tossing a ball softly into the kitchen area and have the student hit soft lift-type dinks back to you. As they begin to hit their dinks consistently, we would gradually feed the ball a bit faster and vary the location. Soon we would get two beginners together, hitting dinks to each other. Eventually, you would include push dinks, add top or underspin, and continue to upgrade the level of difficulty as their skills developed. For beginners, we would follow the same process to teach the volley, ground strokes, lob, smash, serve and return, and so forth. It takes several sessions to help beginners learn the basic shots and the scoring system.

The philosophy of progressing from easy to difficult shots should guide your entire practice session. Using progressions is the primary philosophy of the coaching program developed by the Registry for Pickleball Professionals coaching programs (RPPK, 2024), which equipped me with my coaching certification. Progressions are the basis of the practice sessions used by all the athletes, performance artists, chess masters, and other world-class experts described in the peak performance literature.

Including competitions in practice sessions

The RPPK coaching model also includes the use of "mini competitions" at the end of drill progressions. They represent the most intense type of practice. For example, you can play games to 5, 7, or 11 points with down-the-line or crosscourt dinks, volleys, ground strokes, and even lobs and smashes. The competitions maximize the difficulty level of the drills and encourage a sharp focus of attention. These competitions train you to become accustomed to competitive play and help you feel more confident, become more effective in tournament competition, and be less likely to lose points through nervousness.

Practicing without a partner

Given the importance of practice to improving your skills, you may need to practice when a partner is not available. There are several ways to practice without a coach or partner, such as hitting from a bucket of balls, using a ball machine, or practicing shots against a backboard or wall. With a bucket of balls, you can practice hitting deep serves with topspin near the opponent's baseline. You can set out cones as targets and try to hit them. You can also practice hitting forehand and backhand drives by dropping and hitting the ball.

If you have access to a ball machine, you can work on almost all your strokes even without a partner. You can set the machine to hit forehand and backhand groundstrokes, volleys, third shot drops, lobs, etc. Gallwey (1997), although talking about practicing tennis, recommends using a ball machine (with ball speed set at a high level) to practice volleys and improve your skill as well as reflexes on volleys. He suggests gradually moving the ball machine closer and closer to the net to maximally challenge your reflexes.

My personal favorite for solo practice is hitting against a backboard or wall. I have a wall in my garage that works well for this. I hit down the line dinks, cross court dinks, and down the line and cross courts to work on shots as well as movement and footwork. I usually hit dinks, then volleys, then groundstrokes. For dinks, I hit 30 or so down the line (i.e., forehands or backhands), then cross court going from forehand to backhand, then mix it up. I do the same thing with volleys, hitting 100 forehands, backhands, cross courts, etc. I gradually move closer to the wall to decrease my reaction time and increase the difficulty level. Groundstrokes are next, using the same approach, usually 35 or so shots for each component. I work on both topspin and underspin groundstrokes. (I usually hit serve returns with underspin.) I use progressions and increase the difficulty of each shot by moving closer to the wall or by increasing the angle I hit on cross court shots, forcing me to run faster to reach the ball. I minimize rest time between drills to keep my heart rate up. Total practice time is about 25 minutes. When I'm finished, I feel confident that I'm not going to miss many of these shots the next time I play a game!

You might want to try my approach to practicing or the programs created by professional coaches. I encourage you to check them out. Tyson McGuffin and Kyle McKenzie have developed a number of YouTube videos of drills. CJ Johnson and Tony Roig have numerous drills in their instructional videos. (I have a subscription to their training program). Susannah Barr, an APP Professional affiliated with Selkirk, has developed a number of videos and downloadable handouts that include using tiny foam golf balls instead of pickleballs to increase difficulty levels. She also uses targets and cones, games of "Mortimer," and countless variations of drills involving an array of possible shots.

Personally, I find practicing to be a lot of fun. Because it can be a lot of work, I recommend you reward yourself at the end of your practice sessions. Maybe get a coffee or a treat. Relax in a jacuzzi. Go out to lunch. Looking forward to something positive, help maintain your motivation to practice. It is also highly motivating to see and enjoy how well you play the next time you are on the court for a game!

Practicing off the court - Visualization

You can also practice off the court using visualization; it's a form of mental practice that nicely complements physical, on-court practice. With visualization, our brains process images just like real actions, with similar brain patterns of neural firing even if there is no actual movement involved. Research shows that visualization, like on-court practice, is very effective in creating skill improvement (Knight, 2024). To use visualization, relax and close your eyes, then picture yourself hitting a pickleball shot using exactly the correct form and technique. Envision it with as much detail as possible, what you see, feel, and hear as you hit the shot. Experience the feelings of satisfaction and the resulting positive emotional state (e.g., having fun, feeling excited). You can also visualize yourself playing a game using the strategies you are trying to adopt -- you're hitting serves and returns deep, scurrying up to the NVZ after a return, etc. I particularly like to visualize the defensive game, including the joy of returning impossibly fast smashes and volleys. Bass (2023) emphasized that you always visualize success, be as specific and detailed as possible, and "feel the pressure" you would experience in a competitive situation. I will discuss visualization further in Chapters 5 and 7, addressing ways of improving concentration and reducing competition-related anxiety or limiting beliefs about your performance capabilities.

Summary and Conclusions

Practicing is an essential component of your strategy for moving your game to the next level. Practice moves your skills from the limited, inefficient System 2 functioning into the fast, automatic functioning of System 1. In a game situation, your System 1 skills will be solid and reliable.

Ideally you should practice once or twice a week, for an hour to an hour-and-a-half each session. After a physical warmup and basic stretching, select several skills you want to work on and begin with a challenging one first. Begin at an easy level of difficulty and find ways to quickly increase the difficulty level through pace, placement, spin, etc., so that it is very difficult for you to perform the shot or skill consistently. You will make multiple errors during the drill, which is good! Next, engage in some type of competition with your partner using this drill, perhaps several mini games of 5 or 7 points. After you are finished with the mini games, take a short break for water and rest; then move on to the next drill. Repeat the process, increasing the difficulty level of the next drill until you are again pushed to your limits. Create a competition with this drill. Continue, moving on to new drills, until your practice time is up. Save the shots with which you are most comfortable for last, when you are the most tired and won't need to expend full energy to perform them. The next time you play a competitive game, notice the improvement you are seeing in the shots you have practiced!

Life Lesson

The principles discussed in this chapter can be applied more broadly to our lives outside of pickleball. We can learn pretty much anything that we decide to learn. We might try learning to play a musical instrument, speaking a foreign language, acquiring new computer skills, learning carpentry, or developing auto repair skills. Any time we learn something new, there is an initial phase of System 2 conscious thinking to absorb new information. With time and practice, more of System 1 unconscious, automatic thinking is involved, with much higher information capacity, speed, and reliability. We should incorporate sufficient intensity when we are learning, allow enough time for practice, and make sure we practice the new, hard aspects before we repeat what we already know. Any learning will involve neuroplasticity, creating new neuronal connections and expanding the areas in our brains associated with the activity. Consequently, our ability to perform the new skill will expand as we learn.

While learning any new skill or gaining new knowledge, we may experience several cognitive biases that adversely impact learning. These include the Negativity Bias (tending to focus on mistakes and what is going wrong), Loss Aversion (trying to avoid losing something, when we learn something new, including time for other activities or financial resources), and What You See Is All There Is (WYSIATI, not seeing the full scope or implications of what we are learning). Being aware of these biases, we can limit their potential to slow or derail learning new skills.

In addition, we can experience the "performance paradox" in any area of our life, where simply performing our job, hobbies, other sports, even cooking, without a learning or practice component leads to stagnation and decline. The good news is that it is not necessary to have innate talents or abilities to learn new skills. We just need the desire and willingness to gain new knowledge, and we need to practice!

Chapter Three

Feedback and Tracking

The last chapter focused on how to practice, rehearsing a behavior you are trying to improve until you can perform it properly and automatically. However, practice by itself, without some form of feedback, does not necessarily lead to improvement. Practice must be followed as soon as possible by performance feedback so that needed corrections can be made (Ericsson, 2020). If there is a long delay between actions and feedback, or if the feedback is vague, it is hard to make corrections. Further, the feedback must be accurate, or you may make the wrong corrections. Each time you practice a behavior and get feedback about the outcome, you have created a "feedback loop," the basic unit of all learning. Figure 2 shows the process for creating a feedback loop.

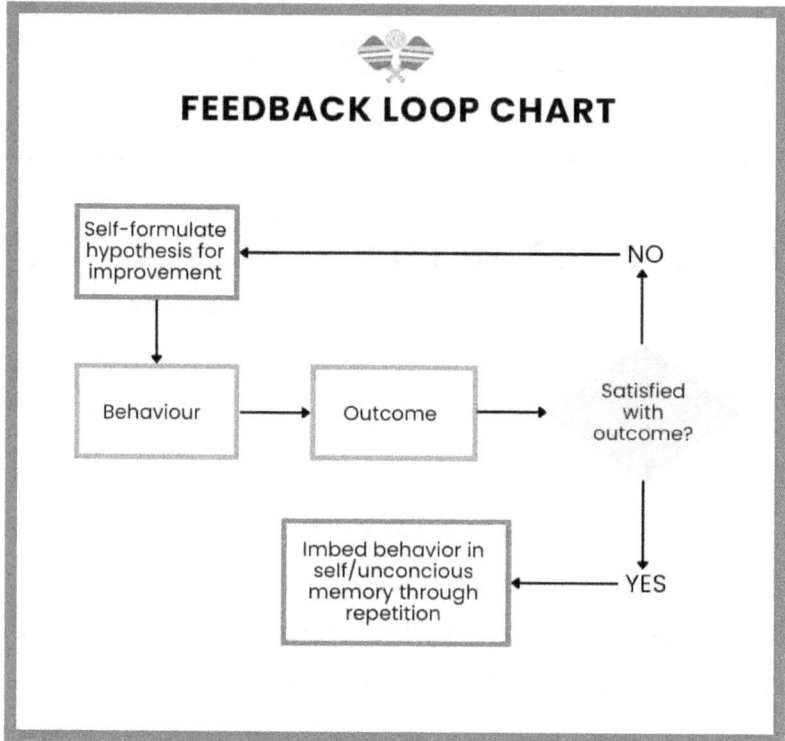

Figure 2. A feedback loop for pickleball

To incorporate feedback into a strategy for improving your game, begin by learning the mechanics of a new shot (e.g., footwork, desired trajectory, spin, paddle grip) . As you practice the shot, observe the outcomes of your practice and use the outcomes as feedback to learn how to improve the shot. Adjust the mechanics of the shot as needed for improvement. While you progress through many iterations of the feedback loop, your shot gets better and better.

This principle works quite well up to a certain point. If you can correctly diagnose the problems with your stroke based on your practice outcomes, the feedback loop works fine. Unfortunately, sometimes you don't know what is wrong with your shot. For example, I've been working on a two-handed backhand, but I really don't know why it's not working. So, without feedback that helps me understand the issue with the way I'm hitting the shot, I can't make needed changes.

As Sayid (2010) struggled to hit increasingly difficult shots during practice sessions, he concluded that merely practicing and trying to improve wasn't sufficient to achieve the advances he wanted for his game. Fortunately, he was able to get immediate feedback from his new Chinese coach that helped him revise his techniques for better outcomes. For example, his coach noticed that Sayid was hitting very "wristy" shots. Although Sayid thought his "wristiness" was an advantage in that it made it hard for his opponents to predict the shot, his coach thought his wristiness introduced troublesome variability in his strokes, leading to unforced errors. His coach worked with him to hit every shot with consistent wrist action, considerably reducing the potential for error. Sayid went from hitting no more than 15 shots in a row without missing to hitting over 200 consecutive shots with reliable precision. "That," said Sayid, "is the power of feedback!"

Similarly, Juncewicz (2017) described the role of feedback in the success of the Chinese Olympic diving team. The Chinese divers had won gold medals in six of eight diving events in the 2012 Olympics and seven of eight events in 2016. Juncewicz concluded that few teams in any sport have dominated to the extent shown by the Chinese. What was the basis for their success? It was feedback! He pointed out that feedback was an integral part of all their practice sessions. After a diver completed a practice dive, he or she would get out of the water and receive immediate feedback from a coach, for every dive, with an emphasis on what could be improved next time. The diver would then walk over to a video screen and view replays of the dive, seeing the performance in person and receiving additional suggestions from the coaches. Juncewicz advised that other performers should use this process too. He suggested they "fall in love with feedback" instead of avoiding it or taking it personally. As with Sayid's experience, feedback was the key to world class performance.

Other performers may not have easy access to immediate feedback and must find creative ways to get it. Juncewicz cites chess as an example where players don't receive feedback about any particular move. They only get win/loss information when the game is over. As a result, they don't know if a particular move was good or bad, or what might have happened in they had moved differently. To rectify the situation, chess players have learned to use post-game studies in lieu of real-time feedback to improve their game moves. The players replicate scenarios of games played in the past by chess masters. They set up the board to represent a certain situation, perhaps an end-game scenario, from a past game and decide what moves or strategies they would have made. They compare their moves and strategies with the actual game played by a chess master, analyzing how their moves differed from the chess master and the outcomes. They ask, what reasoning led the chess master to make a particular move or series of moves? What were the implications? What did the novice players overlook or perhaps misunderstand when choosing their own moves? The analysis serves as valuable feedback on their own strategies and suggests ways to improve their play.

This approach to feedback in chess was used by Laszlo Polgar, a Hungarian educational psychologist, to teach his daughters how to play chess. He was an early advocate of intense practice coupled with immediate feedback to achieve expert performance. He selected chess as a game on which to try out his learning theories only because it has an objective, quantitative performance scoring system (The Elo system), and because high-level performance can't be blamed on luck or the bias of raters (as in diving and figure skating). All three of his daughters became chess grandmasters and won numerous world and national titles, validating his theories about practice with feedback.

In pickleball, as in chess, feedback may be not be immediate or readily available. Once a game is over, you only know whether you won or lost. Points are played in rapid succession, so there isn't much time for reflection after you make an error or a great shot. You may attribute an error to bad luck or the fact that "no one is perfect." If you missed some forehand drives, what specifically was wrong with them? It's not clear. How about the volleys that went right into the net? It's hard to tell why you missed them. Maybe you weren't bending your knees, perhaps you took your eyes off the ball, perhaps your grip was incorrect. There are many possible hypotheses. What strategies did or didn't work in the game? What strategies could you have used but didn't? In short, because there is little immediate, accurate feedback built into the process of a pickleball game, little (if any) learning has occurred. Later sections of this chapter will provide specific strategies for getting the feedback you need to improve.

There is an additional reason why we often get little feedback about our pickleball skills. We don't actively seek it, and we may even avoid getting feedback! In my experience, players rarely ask their partners, opponents, or spectators for feedback about their performance. Think about what would happen if we tried to give our partners feedback about why they made so many mistakes in the last game? What if we tried to explain better strategies they could use? Usually, they get defensive and won't listen, even if we have valuable insights for them.

You will not endear yourself to your partner by giving feedback, unless they ask for it. Even then, you have to be very careful about how you phrase any critical comments. Instead of being a constructive force for improvement, feedback usually generates defensiveness and hostility. Further, the recipient of your feedback may not want to play with you again!

Different forms of feedback can be helpful in advancing our pickleball game to the next level. However, before we consider feedback options, it's helpful to understand the psychological issues related to feedback that make it such a touchy subject.

Psychological biases that make us resistant to feedback

In the last chapter, I introduced the cognitive bias known as "loss aversion" and showed how it applied to several aspects of pickleball, such as reluctance to practice. According to Dittmar (2024), we perceive that we lose valuable playing time if we choose to practice instead, and we further perceive that the loss of playing time outweighs the gains of skill improvement provided by practice. If we do practice, loss aversion also keeps us in our comfort zone and perpetuates the tendency to spend practice time on easy shots we can already hit. By practicing those shots, we avoid losing proficiency in hitting them, but we are not gaining proficiency in hitting more difficult shots if we don't practice them and get the feedback we need to improve. Loss aversion is a big factor in reluctance to practice!

There are several related cognitive biases, reflecting hard-wiring in our brains, that make us resistant to feedback,, including 1) confirmation bias, 2) egocentric bias, 3) sunk cost fallacy bias, and 4) the Dunning-Kruger Effect.

- **Confirmation Bias** is the tendency to pay no attention to things that contradict our beliefs and, likewise, the tendency to attend to things that agree with our beliefs. Encountering information that contradicts our beliefs creates mental stress and tension. It takes a lot of cognitive effort to re-work a basic belief. Ignoring contrary information is much easier than changing long-held beliefs. (Recall that System 2 thinking is very lazy and doesn't like to expend a lot of effort.) In pickleball, suggesting to a hard-hitting player that a soft third shot drop is a more effective strategy will likely result in your being ignored. As another example, many players believe that once you get to the NVZ you should stay there. Suggesting to players that they move backwards a step or two to a better defensive position when the ball is popped up to the opponents is also typically ignored. People won't listen to what they don't want to hear.

- **Egocentric Bias** is the belief that our own point of view is correct and, thus, we don't attend to another person's point of view, especially if it differs from ours. We overestimate our own abilities and over-value our contributions to group projects. We project our beliefs and emotions on others; that is, we see others as having the same feelings about things as we do. In pickleball, we may think our own strategies are the best and that we know best how the game should be played. This makes us very unreceptive to feedback that seems to contradict our own beliefs.

- **Sunk Cost Fallacy** is a bias in which we have invested a great deal of time and energy into something and feel committed to investing even more time and energy to making it work. Although originally intended to explain poor financial investment strategies, this bias applies equally well to why we won't modify how we play our pickleball games. We have invested a lot of time and energy into certain types of shots and strategies. When things go wrong, we tend to "double down" and try harder, rather than to cut our losses and adopt different shots and strategies. Your third shot drive isn't working well against a high-level player? Just hit it harder! You can see that this is a form of loss aversion, where you don't want to lose the time and energy you have invested in a particular shot or strategy, even if it isn't working for you. This bias makes it very difficult to give up strategies and shots that were effective at lower levels of play, but don't work well against higher-level players. The sunk cost fallacy will work against you as you try to move to the next level.

- **The Dunning-Kruger Effect** occurs when people who are relatively unskilled are unaware of their actual skill level, and consequently are overconfident in their abilities. As the saying goes, "we don't know what we don't know." Pickleball players exhibiting the Dunning-Kruger Effect may be relatively new to pickleball but they may feel as though they are experts on the game. Many former tennis players (like myself) are susceptible to this bias. Furthermore, due to the Dunning-Kruger Effect, players aren't able to recognize and appreciate the competency of players with greater skills and so discount their suggestions.

This further increases resistance to feedback. Interestingly, those with higher-level skills or knowledge may exhibit a reverse Dunning-Kruger effect in which they underestimate their skills, being all too conscious of what they still don't know.

In view of the problems associated with confirmation bias, egocentric bias, the sunk cost fallacy, and the Dunning-Kruger effect, it is no wonder that many people are both resistant to feedback and unwilling to actively seek it out. Yet, we have to overcome these biases in order to obtain the feedback we need to improve. We know it's possible to be open to feedback. The pros rely on feedback from coaches and other sources of data in order to persistently improve their games. For a moment, think about your own openness to feedback. Do you ask others for suggestions about your game? Do you ask your partner for feedback? How do you react to other players' suggestions, comments, or even criticism? Have you sought the advice of an expert or higher-level player regarding your strengths and weaknesses as a player? You will struggle to move to a higher level of play if you can't learn to seek out and accept feedback. Not asking others about our performance may be the "safe" way to protect our ego, but it can impede the learning and improvement process we need to move up to the next level of play.

If we can become aware of these biases in our thinking, we will no longer be controlled by them. To correct for possible Confirmation Bias, we should listen to others' comments and consider the truth in their observations and critiques, even if they disagree with what we believe. If we can hold our own beliefs lightly and humbly listen to other points of view, we can sidestep the Egocentric Bias. If we have practiced long and hard on certain shots but they aren't working well in games, we should consciously consider whether we might have invested in a "losing cause" and consider backing off those shots. In this way, we can avoid the Sunk Cost Fallacy. If we are new to the game, we should be open to the possibility that there is much left to learn and listen to the suggestions of more experienced players, thus avoiding the Dunning-Kruger effect. The key is to consider whether we are allowing unconscious biases to interfere with our ability to be receptive to helpful feedback. At the end of the chapter I will return to this issue and describe a mindset that will assist in sidestepping biases and help us remain open to feedback.

Feedback from practice sessions

Practice session and drills can give you immediate feedback about your performance. If you are drilling cross-court dinks and hitting most of them into the net, clearly some corrective action is needed. Like a science experiment, you can hypothesize about what's going wrong and test your hypothesis. For example, if you suspect you're not bending your knees enough, you can try bending your knees more and see if the shot improves. There could be one or many factors contributing to a poor cross-court dink. If you think that the ball needs a higher trajectory, or that you need to watch the ball better, or that you need a more compact swing, you can experiment with each variable to see if you can achieve an improvement. You may have to experiment several times to find the solution. It is likely that you will need to make several changes to really improve the shot. With all the shots you drill in practice, you can try out multiple hypotheses for any issues and experiment with different approaches.

This type of feedback-oriented learning called "deliberate feedback" complements the intensity of deliberate practice as discussed in Chapter 2. It is important to be alert and aware during practice sessions, rather than just hitting a lot of shots on mental autopilot. I have seen and participated in practice sessions involving numerous shots hit without much reflection, awareness, or intensity; and those sessions have resulted in minimal learning or improvement.

Feedback from backboard practice sessions

One reason I like practicing against a backboard is that feedback is immediate. The shot either works or it doesn't. You can easily assess the quality of each shot, and the effects of any changes you make are immediately apparent. As a result, you can quickly test various hypotheses about each shot and very efficiently diagnose issues. Also, in backboard practice sessions, you aren't concerned about your partner's play or erratic shots, so you can focus on your own shots.

I have worked very hard on my cross-court dink shots during my backboard practices, gradually adding more topspin and increasing the pace. I can tell when I'm hitting the shot well and it's a lot of fun! I can imagine how uncomfortable my opponents will be when I hit a high topspin dink to their feet. Through this deliberate practice of my cross-court dinks, I have greatly improved my skill level. It is now my strongest shot.

The same feedback process works with all the other shots I'm practicing. I hit each shot many times, observe the outcomes, and make necessary corrections. With proper corrections, the shots improve until I'm satisfied. I keep hitting improved shots until the changes become automatic, which usually requires multiple practice sessions. I have learned new behaviors for each improved shot, perhaps bending my knees more, hitting a higher trajectory, adding topspin, aiming for particular spots. When I work on my volleys, I know that if I'm not hitting the volley solidly, I won't be able to sustain 100 volleys without a miss, which is my practice goal. Since new learning initially involves a cognitive, factual aspect, I keep a notebook with notes that provide valuable feedback on what I have learned in each practice session. With this feedback and repeated practice, behavior moves to the automatic realm.

Feedback from coaches and observers

The on-court drills and backboard practice sessions are essentially "trial-and-error learning" in which you learn from your mistakes. This type of learning can be very effective, but it may not always be efficient. You might think you have really improved the topspin on your forehand, but like the example of Sayid the table tennis player, you could be using too much wrist and learning an unreliable shot. For example, at one point I thought hitting a hard, flat shot return of a serve was a good idea. I thought it put pressure on the server. As it turned out, all it did was ensure I couldn't get to the NVZ before the server's next shot! I was only hurting myself! I was taking a class from Kyle McKenzie this spring and he pointed out that issue. He told me to hit a slow, higher trajectory shot deep to the baseline to give me a lot more time to reach the NVZ and secure a strategically strong position.

The problem is that needed corrections may not be intuitively obvious and so they don't occur to us. For example, the "pinch the middle" strategy in dinking never occurred to me. I tended to move near the sidelines so I could cover the angle shots. As my coach Carney Lucas pointed out, moving near the center line at appropriate times meant I could take opponents' dinks out of the air more easily, reducing opponents' response times and setting up a put away down the middle.

I much prefer figuring things out on my own, but this is not a good strategy for moving up a level! Not being more open to outside feedback has definitely slowed my improvement efforts. Each time I have a lesson with Carney, he points out areas for improvement that were a complete surprise to me. It is clear that I have a number of "blind spots" to my game where I need outside help to improve. For example, when hitting volleys to opponents who are in the transition zone, I've usually tried to hit the ball at their feet to keep them from coming to the net. Carney has pointed out that those shots are a lot easier for opponents to return than shots hit to their knees or shins which force them to take the ball in the air! Half volleys aren't that difficult, but taking a ball in the air near my feet is much harder! Try it yourself. Try hitting a low volley from deep in the transition zone and see for yourself how hard you have to work to get the ball over the net and how difficult it is to control. It's absurdly difficult!

Furthermore, Carney has urged me watch the body language of my opponents during rallies and be aware of when I've got them backed up or off-balance. At that vulnerable point, I can step up and hit a more aggressive shot. Using only trial-and-error learning, I would never in a million years have thought to do this. When I focus narrowly on watching the ball (great idea, right?), I don't have a sufficiently broad focus to see my opponents' position and stance. Carney is encouraging me to see the ball and, at the same time, be aware of the position and balance of my opponents. Yikes! This is still a work in progress for me, but at least with greater awareness I can practice and improve.

If you don't have a coach, you can seek feedback from friends and acquaintances, asking for their observations and suggestions about your game. Ideally, they would be players performing at a higher level than you. In my experience it is somewhat rare that a player asks others for feedback. It is outside the comfort zone for many people, yet vital to our improvement efforts. Juncewicz (2017) suggests we ask for feedback from people we know will be blunt and honest, perhaps even people who don't like us, such as competitors or rivals. The faster and more frequently you can get feedback, the faster your game will improve. Juncewicz recommends that, instead of avoiding feedback or taking it personally, fall in love with it and use it as insight into future improvement.

Video recording your drilling sessions and games

A great way to get more feedback and data about your game is to set up your cell phone or a video camera on a tripod and record your practice sessions or games. I have recorded several of my games and gained a lot of useful information. I admit, I was initially disappointed to see how slow and awkward I looked. However, the recordings prompted me to add more footwork and movement drills to my workout sessions and this has been very helpful. As described in detail in the next section, video recordings allow you to create quantitative feedback to complement qualitative observations. For example, by reviewing a recording of your games, you can assess how many errors you typically make per game, determine the types of errors you are most prone to making, assess your ability to get to the NVZ after serves and returns, and more.

Using a charting tool to quantify and track your performance

Without using some kind of charting tool or tracking measures, there is no way to know if you are getting better, leading to slower progress and delays in reaching your goal of higher-level play. Using tracking measures can help you identify which aspects of your improvement activities are working and which are not, so they can be modified over time. You will make better decisions and move forward faster.

Tracking can almost automatically improve performance. For examples, research has shown that just keeping track of food intake and exercise leads to weight loss, without any form of intentional dieting or exercising (see Fletcher, 2021). For me, knowing that I'm getting to the NVZ only 30% of the time after returning serve is a great motivator to get up there in a hurry! Tracking my total unforced errors per game has been very helpful in getting more consistent, without any particular behavior change.

As mentioned earlier, games tend to whiz by so fast you aren't able to get good feedback. A great solution is to chart a sample of your games. This involves recording some of your games, coding each point to capture the shot-making and strategies, and computing some basic statistics to evaluate your performance. It is very unlikely that you have ever charted even a single one of your games. I've conducted online searches and talked with knowledgeable coaches and players, but I have never come across a single pickleball charting tool.

Thus, drawing on my career as an organizational psychologist, I have developed a charting tool that may be helpful to your improvement strategy. In my profession, I often developed tools for charting and measuring individual and team performance. I was intrigued to see if I could adapt and apply these techniques to charting pickleball performance. Two years ago, I started looking at various approaches to charting pickleball games. Frankly, I struggled to find an approach that wasn't too complicated or confusing. I almost gave up several times. Finally, a few months ago, I developed a potential workable approach. At first I tried to capture too much data on everything -- serves, returns, reaching the NVZ, types of errors, etc. for both players on a team. It proved too difficult to capture this much data. Thus, I simplified the format to gather less data, while focusing on key areas of performance. Table 1 provides the charting tool I currently use to collect data, analyze a game, and suggest improvement actions. A blank version of the charting form is provided in Appendix A. I encourage you to make copies of the charting tool in Appendix A and use it to chart your own games.

The chart captures five aspects of each point: 1) service and return depth, 2) use of a third shot drop versus a drive, 3) whether the team reached the NVZ after a service return, 4) the number of non-returnable shots (by your team and the opponents), and 5) errors (by your team and the opponents). Service points and return points are coded in different columns to analyze these two aspects separately. I intentionally did not code whether the serving team reached the NVZ or not, since that might take several shots, and the point could be over before they had an opportunity to get to the net.

Table 1. Pickleball charting tool (A guide for the blank form in Appendix A)

Metric #	Statistic Name	A. Your Team Service Points	B. Your Team Return Points
1	Percent of deep serves/returns (ball lands in rear 25% of court)	(If yes-slows returner from reaching NVZ)	(If yes-keeps serving team back, lets you get to NVZ)
2	3rd Shot drives versus drops (3rd shot drop=1, drive=2)	(Are you getting a good mix of drives and drops?)	N/A
3	Your Team Reached NVZ after the return? (Y/N)	N/A	(Creates strategic advantage)
4	Your Team hit a Non-returnable Shot? (Y/N)	POINT FOR YOUR TEAM	(No points won or lost; 2nd server or sideout)
5	Your Team Made an Error (count or code type of error)	(No points lost)	POINT FOR OPPONENTS
6	Opponents hit a non-returnable shot? (Y/N)	(No points lost)	POINT FOR OPPONENTS
7	Opponents made an error? (Y/N)	POINT FOR YOUR TEAM	(No points won or lost)

The chart in Table 1 has notes in each "cell" about the significance of the cell data to the game's outcome. The notes serve as instructions for completing the blank charting form in Appendix A. You code the game from the perspective of your team, coding service points and return points in separate columns. Column A codes the points as they occur on your serve. Column B codes points as they occur on the return of a serve. Your team gets points while serving by either hitting a non-returnable shot or by getting your opponents to make an error. Your opponents earn points in Column B when your team makes an error on a service return point or when your they hit a non-returnable shot.

To code a game using the chart, first video record a game using your cell phone or a video camera. Then view the recording of the game point by point. I've found it works best to view the first point, stop the recording, code what happened in the first point on the chart, and then resume recording for the second point. There is actually a lot of data to record for each point, so be careful that you don't get overwhelmed or fall behind in your coding. Assuming your team serves first, follow this sequence of steps to code information about the first point:

- Code (cell 1A) whether your team served the ball deep to the opponents receiving box. If your serve fell into the farthest 25% (rear quarter), then code a "Y"; if not code an "N". This is somewhat subjective. You have to guess a bit here.

- Code whether your team then hit a 3rd shot drop (1) or a third shot drive (2) using box 2A. (Only coded on service points)

- If your team hit a non-returnable shot to win the first point, enter "1" in cell 4A.

- If your team made an error during the point, enter "1" in cell 5A.

- If your opponents hit a non-returnable shot during the rally, enter "1" in cell 6A.

- If your opponents made an error during the point, enter "1" in cell 7A.

You have captured the key events of the first point by coding these boxes! Code all of your team's serving points in the same way. For receiving points, code the same categories, using Column B instead of A. There are separate columns for serving and receiving points so you can calculate performance statistics for service and return points separately.

Table 2 provides an example of a game that has been coded using the chart, showing a game where "your team" lost 9-11. There are a number of statistics that can be computed with this data, but first let's take a quick overall look. A few things are immediately apparent.

First, only about 57% of your team's serves were deep (13 of 23), landing in the rear 25% of the court. That is, your team's serves lacked depth, setting up relatively easy returns and allowing the opposing team returner to get to the NVZ immediately and, consequently, keeping your serving team pinned to the baseline. Your odds of winning the point when the other team is at the NVZ and you are at the baseline is less than 25%!

Table 2. Example of data for a coded pickleball game			
Metric #	Statistic Name	A. Your Team Service Points	B. Your Team Return Points
1	Percent of deep serves/returns (ball lands in rear 25% of court)	YYYNNNNYNYNYYNNYY YYYYNN (Y=13, N=10)	YYYNNNNYNYNYNNYYNNN NNNNN (Y=8, N=16)
2	3rd Shot drives versus drops (3rd shot drop=1, drive=2)	12221122221122221222 22 (1=6, 2=17)	N/A
3	Your Team Reached NVZ after the return? (Y/N)	N/A	YYYYNNNYYNYNYNYNYYYN NYYY (Y=15, N=9)
4	Your Team hit a Non-returnable Shot (Y/N)	111 (3 total)	11111 (5 total)
5	Your Team Made an Error (count or code type of error)	11111111 (8 total)	1111111 (7 total)
6	Opponents hit a non-returnable shot (Y/N)	111111 (6 total)	1111 (4 total)
7	Opponents made an error (Y/N)	111111 (6 total)	11111111 (8 total)

Second, your team's serve returns also lacked depth, with only about 32% (8 deep, 16 short) of the returns landing deep. Consequently, the opposing serving team would have an easy time getting to the NVZ, neutralizing the advantage your team should have by controlling the net. Your opponents likely would win many more points thanks to your short service return, compared to fewer points if you had kept them pinned to the baseline!

Third, notice that your team, when serving, hit almost no 3rd shot drops (6 out of 23, 14.3%), relying on drives almost exclusively. This is not an effective strategy for quickly getting to the NVZ and having a good chance to win the point! It is not the mix of shots you would typically see in a 4.5+ team. When combined with your short serves, your team is essentially giving away a high percentage of service points, other things being equal.

Fourth, your team made 15 errors this game, 8 while serving and 7 while returning; your opponents made only 14 errors, which is also quite high. However, not all errors are equal in impact. You can make a million errors while serving, and it won't cost you a single point, but each error you make while receiving costs you 1 point. You are making way too many errors in one game! The 7 errors you made on their serve plus their 4 non-returnable shots gave them 11 points to win the game.

These four factors alone suggest you basically handed the game to the opponents. In the end, your team only lost 11-9. Correcting any one of these factors may easily have led to a win. Correcting all four may have resulted in thoroughly defeating your opponents!

What actionable changes to your strategy and shot making would the chart suggest? First, your team should set up some drilling sessions and work hard on hitting deep serves and deep returns. The deep serves will slow the returner's approach to the NVZ and give your team more time to get to the NVZ. You should also practice getting to the NVZ after hitting your 3rd shot and create an intention to get to the NVZ as soon as possible.

Another actionable change involves your choice of a 3rd shot. It appears that your team avoided the 3rd shot drop like the plague! This suggests you need to drill the 3rd shot drop until you can hit it reliably and have confidence to use it in a game. It should be an integral part of your strategy.

In addition, your team needs to practice getting to the NVZ after service returns, with a goal of getting there 100% of the time. You will win a much higher percentage of points while planted at the NVZ! You should also try to pin your opponents at the baseline through deep volleys and make it very difficult for them to move up.

Lastly, your team needs to make a conscious attempt to reduce the number of unforced errors. The 15 total was way too high. Research has shown that 75% of all pickleball points end with an error. You can win a lot of games simply by being aware of the error count and keeping it to a minimum. I see countless points lost by overhitting volleys, for example. Hitting high volleys at 3/4 pace would significantly reduce the number of errors and still win most points. If you can slow your shots down a bit and be a little less aggressive, you will make far fewer unforced errors. Personally, I set a goal of hitting four or fewer errors per game. If I'm above that goal, I slow down the ball and choose less risky shots. You should determine what causes your team's errors and make needed corrections. Are you making errors due to nerves, lack of concentration, hitting too hard, going for low percentage shots?

Drill on the shots you're missing, slow down the ball until you're more consistent; be determined to play more consistently.

There is something of a learning curve to recording and charting your games. It certainly takes time and discipline. Nevertheless, there are big payoffs from recording and charting, in terms of accelerating your efforts to more quickly move to the next level. If you keep an archive of the recordings and charts, you can objectively assess your improvements over time.

Finally, note that coding just one game can be somewhat unreliable, statistically, due to the small sample size of shots. I recommend coding multiple games, say four or five, and combining the data before you compute the statistics. The data and resulting statistics will then be more truly representative of your game performance.

Learn from Failure

As you begin to seek feedback about your performance and to track your game performance, you will experience repeated instances of failures. In a game situation you might find yourself hitting many of those 3rd shot drops you've been practicing into the net or setting up easy put-aways for your opponents. This is actually good news! The errors show that you're pushing beyond your comfort zone, trying new behaviors. You can't realistically expect to succeed every time as you are developing your game.

Michael Jordan once said in a famous Nike commercial, "I've missed more than 9,000 shots in my career. I've lost almost 300 games; 26 times I've been trusted to take the last shot and missed. I've failed over and over again in life and that is why I succeed." Jordan may have missed more final shots than anyone else, but he also *made* more game-winning shots than anyone else.

A number of writers (e.g., Ericsson, 2016; Quick, 2020) believe that *failure is the key to success* and that fear of failure is a recipe for stagnation. Your goal in trying to improve your pickleball game is to "fail early, fail fast, and fail often" and to "fall in love with failure" (Juncewicz, 2017).

However, it is important to learn something from failures. If you were hitting the 3rd shot drop into the net, why was that happening? Perhaps you weren't bending your knees and lifting up on the shot. Perhaps the trajectory was too low. Maybe you were fearful of overhitting and hit too softly. As we have emphasized before, you need to recognize failures, hypothesize what went wrong, and try out new behaviors until you have found a good solution. Therefore, failures are just a sign you are on the road to improvement, and it's important to celebrate them as well as your successes!

Life Lesson

Anything we learn in life involves a feedback loop, with early conscious learning leading to behavior followed by outcomes, with feedback about the outcomes informing our learning process. We may be learning carpentry skills or trying to improve our computer programming ability to further our career goals. Regardless of what we are learning, the learning becomes less conscious and more automatic as we progress.

We need to practice the new skills and behaviors and to receive immediate and accurate feedback to make the learning process more efficient, yet most of us avoid the feedback we need. We resist practicing isolated aspects of the new skill because it seems like a lot of work and just takes us away from using the actual skills we are learning (the bias of "loss aversion"). We resist getting feedback about our performance due to the cognitive biases of Confirmation Bias (we don't want to get information that contradicts what we already think), Egocentric Bias (we think we are right), Sunk Cost Fallacy (we don't want to think we've wasted our time and effort doing the wrong thing), and the Dunning-Kruger Effect (as beginners, we overestimate our level of performance). Our learning will be much more efficient, in the long run, if we can overcome these biases and welcome feedback about our performance. We need to learn to welcome mistakes and failures, not take them personally, and see negative outcomes as a sign that we are pushing our limits and trying to learn something new.

Chapter Four

The Skills You Need for the Next Level

So far in this book we have discussed two major barriers to your moving to the next level of play, including the lack of practice and feedback. Chapter 2 discussed the issue of insufficient practice and how to overcome it with regular, intense practice sessions focused on the most difficult aspects of your game. Chapter 3 discussed the negative effects of lack of immediate and accurate feedback on performance and how to get the crucial information you need to correct errors and improve your shots and strategies. In this chapter, I will discuss 1) identifying and incorporating the new shots, skills, and strategies needed for next-level play into your game and 2) using drills and activities to help you acquire these skills.

Why you may not know what's needed at the next level

Why is there even a need for this chapter? I believe players are often unaware of what's needed at the next level, therefore, they are "unaware that they are unaware." Here are some reasons why this is true. First, it's likely you play mainly with players of your own skill level or lower, so you are getting little exposure to higher-level shots and strategies. In this case, you have a limited appreciation for the intricacies of higher-level play. For example, if you are a 3.5-level player, you likely see very few 3rd shot drops and few good quality dinks, and you have not learned about the tactics and strategies built around these shots. Instead, you probably see a lot of drives and hard volleys. You have little opportunity to engage in observational learning (Bandura, 1997) which is a rapid, efficient approach to learning new skills almost unconsciously. In observational learning you learn new skills simply by watching others attentively, coding the new skills into your memory, and recall and apply them later yourself. Observational learning can be a very fast and efficient way of learning complex new skills.

In addition to having limited exposure to higher-level play, it's likely that no one has explained to you the demands of the next level, which can actually be very difficult to articulate. In Dittmar Laido's book *The Art of Practice* (2024), he describes the difficulty he encountered in discovering the secrets of top circus performers. He wanted to know how they gained their expertise. When he asked them in interviews, they shared comments like "you do what you love" or "you work hard," but they were unable to explain exactly what they were doing that made them top performers. They were not attempting to hide their performance secrets from Dittmar, they just couldn't articulate what they were doing differently. Dittmar ultimately relied on observation of their practice sessions and performances to identify their effective learning strategies.

There is a good reason the top performers couldn't explain why they excelled. Complex skills are stored in System 1 unconscious memories and are habits that are not readily accessible to System 2 conscious awareness. Their performances are complex and nearly automatic.

Given that expert skills are largely automatic habits and not verbalized, System 2 awareness can't articulate them. Dittmar pointed out that many top performers in any area (sports, music, research, literature) are likewise unable to explain what they do and how it is different from average performers. This is true of pickleball as well. If you ask higher-level players to explain what you need to do to reach the next level, they may be unable to give you an answer you can act on.

Several cognitive biases also make it difficult to become aware of the existence of higher-level skills. One such bias is the WYSIATI (What You See Is All There Is) bias. In Chapter 2 we described WYSIATI as occurring when players at any given level use a limited range of shots and tactics at their level of play and believe that these shots and tactics represent the entire range of pickleball skills. The shots they see are all there is. Another way of saying this is "we don't know what we don't know." Thus, we might think that what is needed to move up to a higher level is just to hit our current shots better, or harder. In this bias, we jump to a false conclusion based on very little evidence. Given that we have limited exposure to higher level play and that higher-level players have not articulated the new requirements to us, System 1 concludes we don't need to do anything new. System 2, reluctant to waste mental energy (i.e., subject to laziness), is unwilling to challenge these conclusions without a good reason. We remain oblivious to the new requirements of higher-level play.

Another bias that keeps us from seeing the need for new shots is Selective Attention. This bias reflects the brain's limited ability to process and absorb all the vast amount of incoming information. To deal with the continual feed of incoming information, the brain filters the information and directs our attention to what it thinks is important, based on our interests, past experiences, goals, and emotions (Wood, 2024). Consequently, as we watch higher-level players, we may see familiar shots and strategies, but we overlook and dismiss unfamiliar elements. This is like the classic social psychology "Invisible Gorilla Experiment" (Chabris and Simons, 1999) in which research participants watched a video of a basketball game and were instructed to count the number of passes the players made. While counting passes, the participants completely overlooked an actor dressed as a gorilla who walked right through the scene, beat his chest with both fists, and left. How does the gorilla study apply to pickleball? As a beginner, we may focus on the basics of pickleball and be completely oblivious to many of the things a more advanced player is doing. We may see a good forehand drive, but not notice the drop shots or dinks that were delivered. When I was just starting out as a 3.0-level player, I remember being vaguely puzzled by the 3rd shot drops and dinks I saw advanced players use. I didn't know why they hit such soft shots when they could hit the ball harder. Now, as a 4.5-level player, I'm often amazed that players at the 3.5 level can be oblivious to the need for 3rd shot drops and good dinks and instead be focused on hitting hard drives and volleys. Due to attention bias, they are simply unable to see and process some higher-level aspects of the game.

The point I am trying to make is that, for a number of good reasons, we are likely to be ignorant of the shots, skills, and strategies needed at the next level. So, how can we practice and learn these new skills if we don't know what they are?

Identifying what you need for the next level

In the next section, A Summary of Characteristics for Each Level, I summarize the "skills and drills" needed to reach each level of pickleball play from 2.5 to 5.5. A more complete description of the skills and drills is provided in Appendix B.

I drew from a number of sources in developing the lists of skills and drills needed for each level. has lists of the criteria for each level, which are used in rating player skill levels and defining each level of play. There are also helpful YouTube videos that compare specific levels with the next higher level. I recommend the videos by Joey Gmuer in his series. They are informative and hilarious as well! I encourage you to find the Joey Gmuer video that compares your own level with the next higher level and watch it ASAP, taking notes on his comments. The website also has valuable articles on skill levels and the differences between levels.

I suggest this sequence of steps for identifying the skills you need for the next level.

- Read the summary of skills needed for your next level of play, which is included in the next section of this Chapter.

- Find the Appendix section that provides full details of the skills and drills needed for your next level. As you read the Appendix, take notes on the areas you need to improve in your game. Identify the drills that are relevant to gaining these skills.

- Watch the Joey Gmuer video on YouTube that discusses your goal level. Take notes on his comments. Laugh regularly.

- Begin incorporating the drills into your practice sessions.

- Start incorporating the new skills in your game play.

A summary of characteristics for each level

The following sections provide a brief overview of the skills and strategies needed at each level of pickleball play, from 2.5 to 5.5+. (I didn't include the 2.0 level because it's really not a level people aspire to achieve.)

Characteristics of 2.5-level players

The 2.5-level players have relatively little experience on the court and a limited understanding of the basic rules and gameplay. They can serve with some consistency, hitting the ball with little power or spin, and placement may still be erratic. They can execute basic shots (e.g., forehand and backhand shots) if the ball is within their reach and not hit too hard. They struggle to hit volleys and often miss dinks. They have a basic understanding of court positioning and may attempt to move to the non-volley zone. They do not move well with their partners and may leave large gaps between themselves and their partner on the court. They have only begun to understand basic strategy. The 2.5-level players generally understand the scoring system and can keep score. At this level, their focus should be on developing basic consistency, understanding the rules, and enjoying the game. They should engage in regular practice and play with others to gain experience and comfort on the court. (Note: A detailed list of skills and appropriate drills for moving to the 2.5 level is provided in Appendix B)

Characteristics of 3.0-level players

Those playing at the 3.0-level have gained more experience and confidence on the court compared to beginners. They know the basic rules, techniques, and strategies of pickleball. They have improved court coverage, compared to a 2.5 player, but they do not have sufficient experience to anticipate where their opponents' shots will land. They have consistent serves, with some degree of placement and variety, but they may lack depth, spin, and placement. They often fail to get to the NVZ after a return of serve. They can hit dinks and volleys if the ball is hit within their reach and without too much pace or spin, but they may lack control and make frequent errors. They have not learned to hit a 3rd shot drop. They can hit lobs, but they lob too frequently and lack placement skills. Rallies at this level may be short, with many balls hit too high above the net for easy put aways. They cannot sustain volley exchanges. They are comfortable with the scoring process and can keep track of the score. The 3.0-level players demonstrate more consistency, better shot control, and a deeper understanding of the game compared than 2.5-level players, who are still in the early stages of developing their skills and game knowledge. (Note: A detailed list of skills and appropriate drills for moving to the 3.0 level is provided in Appendix B.)

Characteristics of 3.5-level players

The 3.5-level players can serve effectively, hitting deep serves and placing the ball deep and into the backhand corner. They can comfortably sustain longer rallies. Their forehands are typically much stronger than their backhands, and their forehands may be formidable weapons during the game. Few 3.5-level players have a consistent backhand drive. Players at this level typically make frequent unforced errors, often due to overly aggressive shot selection. They may not always get to the NVZ after a serve return. They have generally not mastered the drop shot, due to lack of practice and/or interest, and, thus, they avoid hitting it. They can hit forehand and backhand dinks, although the dinks will typically not be as well-placed as those of higher-level players, they dinks will be hit with frequent errors.

These players tend to hit with considerable power and aggressiveness, resulting in many errors. They generally have solid volleys but rely on power and rarely attempt to reset into a dinking game. At the NVZ, they often fail to anticipate when their opponents' drives will go out and hit them anyway, often giving away a free point. They generally have good lobs, but they may hit them too often or inappropriately, setting up smashes by the other team. They may have good overheads but may not hit with enough angle or pace to put the ball away immediately. They may fail to recognize and exploit an opponent's weaknesses (especially backhands), although they may target more shots to the weaker opponent. The level of athleticism of the 3.5 player is often quite high. Many 3.5 players were athletes in school and have maintained strength, fitness, and mobility. (Note: A detailed list of skills and appropriate drills for moving to the 3.5 level is provided in Appendix B.)

Characteristics of 4.0-level players

The 4.0-level players demonstrate improved consistency in their shots compared to 3.5 players. They make far fewer drive, volley, and dinking errors. They show more advanced strategic thinking. They can serve the ball deep with spin, targeting the backhand side. As returners, they try to keep the serving team from reaching the NVZ through effective returns and 4th shots. They try to keep their opponents off balance and capitalize on opponents' poor positioning. They are aware of their opponents' strengths and weaknesses, selecting the opponent with the weaker 3rd shot drop for serve returns and frequently targeting the weaker opponent. They know when to deploy power shots versus soft shots against their opponents, and they can play the soft game when needed. They have good stroke mechanics on forehand drives, volleys, dinks, and drop shots but may still lack some consistency on backhand shots. They can control the height and pace of dinks better than 3.5-level players but may lack the top or underspin necessary for aggressive dinking. They may end dinking rallies too soon, going for a speedup prematurely.

They may still lack effective drop shot skills and focus instead on 3rd shot drives, resulting in unforced errors and difficulty getting to the NVZ. They can engage in rapid hand battles at the NVZ and are able to defend against some hard-hit volleys and overheads, although they lack the more comprehensive defensive skills of the 4.5-level player. Many 4.0-level players fail to move back a step or two when in a defensive position at the net. They can get to the NVZ after a serve return but may not get there consistently. Due to a weak 3rd shot drop, they have trouble getting to the NVZ when serving and may rely on drives during serving points. They can shift between low-, medium-, and high-paced shots more easily than 3.5-level players. Players at the 4.0 level are generally quite athletic, with good strength, speed, and flexibility. They have overcome many of the performance weaknesses listed for the 3.5-level player, especially in the areas of consistency and ability to use both a soft and a power game.

(Note: A detailed list of skills and appropriate drills for moving to the 4.0 level is provided in Appendix B.)

Characteristics of 4.5-level players

The 4.5-level players are more consistent in shot execution, compared to the 4.0-level players, and they can use power more effectively to create offensive situations. They have good control over dink shots, varying depth and speed to create opportunities. They can sustain long dinking rallies and attack opponents' dinks that are too high or deep. They demonstrate more deliberate and strategic shot selection and better placement than lower-level players. They have mastered various 3rd shot choices and strategies, consistently executing both drop shots and drives from both forehand and backhand sides. They are comfortable with advanced volley techniques, including blocking hard volleys, adding topspin to drop the volley low over the net, and hitting powerful swinging volleys. They exhibit a high level of strategic play, working more effectively with their partners and adapting their game plan based on opponents' strengths and weaknesses. They display excellent footwork as well as quick movement and efficient weight transfer, allowing for better court coverage. They have developed a higher level of variety, depth, and pace in their serves and returns. They have a deeper understanding of the strategies of the serving and return games, effective court positioning, use of power versus control, and the ability to read opponents effectively. These differences, collectively, contribute to a more refined and competitive level of play for 4.5-level players compared to those at the 4.0 level. (Note: A detailed list of skills and appropriate drills for moving to the 4.5 level is provided in Appendix B.)

Characteristics of 5.0-level level players

The 5.0-level players demonstrate significantly higher consistency and control in all aspects of their game compared to the 4.5-level player. They use more aggressive serves with deeper placement, more spin, and better variety. Their returns are also deeper, including heavy slice to keep the ball low and bouncing low, and they are able to keep opponents off balance. They excel at a variety of 3rd shot drops and drives, placing the 3rd shot drop in a variety of locations. Their 3rd shot drives are very low over the net, powerful, and very difficult to return. They aggressively attack 4th shots from the NVZ, hitting the ball deep to their opponents' feet, making it very difficult for the serving team to get to the NVZ and, thus, maintaining the returning team net position advantage. They hit punishing volleys, often hitting non-returnable shots.

They make few errors in dinking exchanges, dinking aggressively and deeply to the feet of their opponents. They create and capitalize on offensive opportunities during these rallies. They demonstrate advanced strategic thinking, often planning several shots ahead and adapting their game plan to their opponents' strengths and weaknesses. They have fast hand speed and good anticipation, allowing them to react more quickly to their opponents' shot and to take charge of hand battle at the net. They can return and reset powerful volleys and overheads that appear to be winners for the other team. They can handle the increased pressure and pace of high-level play, maintaining their performance in challenging situations. They display superior court coverage and athleticism, allowing them to reach and return difficult shots that lower-level players could not hope to return. (Note: A detailed list of skills and appropriate drills for moving to the 5.0 level is provided in Appendix B.)

Characteristics of 5.5+ level players

The 5.5+ level players have near-perfect consistency and precision in all aspects of their game, exceeding the shot execution of 5.0-level players. They consistently win or place highly in major tournaments, even achieving victories against top professionals. They have mastered every possible pickleball skill, and they often have their own unique approach to difficult shots. There may be very few players who can go toe-to-toe with 5.5+ level players; many players at this level are professional or semi-professional players. They have an extremely advanced understanding of strategy and can adapt their game plan instantly. The transition from the 5.0 to the 5.5+ level represents the difference between very skilled amateur players and top professional competitors. The 5.5+ level rating is reserved for elite players in the sport who consistently perform at the highest levels of competition. (Note: A listing of skills for the 5.5+ level is provided in Appendix B.)

After reviewing the summary of your desired level, be sure to review the detailed descriptions and lists of appropriate drills provided in the appropriate Appendix. I suggest you use a notebook to write down the desired skills and strategies you need to acquire and begin to track your progress towards the next level. Include a list of the things you need to stop doing, such as over-hitting or making too many errors. Document which drills you are working on and make notes about your progress.

Effective strategies common to all levels of play

While developing the lists of skills for each level, I realized that some important shots and strategies are common to all levels. It seemed redundant to list them for each level separately. Therefore, I have developed a list of shots and strategies with cross-level commonality, drawing from articles by Betsy Kenniston (2023), Staci Townsend (2021), and my own observations. Regardless of your desired level of play, you should incorporate the following suggestions into your improvement plan.

1. Serve deep to the backhand corner.

2. Return deep to the weaker opponent (or the one with the weaker 3rd shot). Consider using underspin on your returns and get to the NVZ before the serving team hits their 3rd shot if you can.

3. Always watch the ball closely; try to see the ball hit the paddle, even pausing momentarily to let the paddle follow through. Try to see the holes in the ball as it approaches you. Look up only after you have hit the shot, except for reflex volleys at the net, when there is not enough time to see the ball hit the paddle.

4. Return to "ready" position immediately (no hesitation) after hitting a shot.

5. Play to your own strengths; identify and exploit your opponents' weaknesses.

6. Stay patient, do not overhit.

7. Count the errors you make in each game and try to keep your errors to a minimum (aim for four or fewer errors in a game).

8. Hit the pickleball low over the net on your drives.

9. Always communicate with your partner, move together, and avoid separation.

10. When at the NVZ, let balls go out (chest high or higher).

11. Mostly dink crosscourt but hit speedups to the opponent across from you. Do not hit speedups crosscourt or you will annoy your partner.

12. Mostly hit down the middle.

13. Lob less than you'd prefer.

14. Hit a 3rd shot drop regularly, often to the opponents' backhands.

15. Aim for opponents' feet or shins with your volleys and overheads.

16. Take dinks out of the air if you can.

17. Be aware of your opponents' position and balance on the court. Hit at opponents who are off balance or out of position, e.g., hit behind your opponent.

18. Learn a compact stroke for efficiency and quickness.

Using the Pareto principle to help identify key areas for improvement

You may have a fairly long list of strategies for advancing to the next level. If so, I suggest that you narrow the list to four or five of the most important issues and focus on these strategies first. When I was working on multiple ways to improve my game, and not focusing on anything very well, I thought about the Pareto principle, or the 80/20 rule, and its application to pickleball. The Pareto Principle states that 80% of outcomes result from 20% of the inputs (Simmons, 2020), so that a minority of effort leads to a majority of results. Here are some examples:

- In businesses, 20% of customers account for 80% of the profits.

- In software development, 20% of the programming errors lead to 80% of the software problems.

- You likely wear 20% of the clothes in your closet 80% of the time.

- You likely order 20% of the items on a menu 80% of the time.

- In pickleball, 80% of your errors are likely the result of 20% of your shots.

In any situation there are some things that are inherently more important and have a bigger impact than others. In pickleball, just a few of your shots are causing the majority of your errors. Thus, just a few critical changes to your game can have a significant impact on your performance and outcomes, while changes in other areas may have relatively little impact.

This means it's important to use our limited resources most efficiently to move to the next level. Applying the Pareto principle, we should focus on the critical 20% of the shots and strategies holding us back. This is actually very good news, because it means making a few critical changes to our game will result in outsized, disproportionate improvements! Making a few key corrections might, in fact, be all we need to do to move to the next level. We just need to ensure we are correcting the right ones. For example, I can think of several good 3.5-level players who would be 4.0-level players immediately if they hit the ball with slightly less power (to reduce unforced errors) or if they incorporated a 3rd shot drop into their repertoire. Many players would improve immediately if they got returned to a ready position right after hitting a shot.

I have applied the Pareto principle to my own game and identified a few key areas for improvement, as I try to solidify my play at the 4.5 level. My Pareto items include the following.

- Significantly reduce the number of errors per game. Before each shot, I mentally tell myself that I'm going to get the ball "in" no matter what. I also count the number of errors I make in a game. If I'm making too many errors, I need to regain concentration and play a more consistency-oriented game. For me, I'm achieving good performance if I make four or fewer errors in a game; five to nine errors is an indicator of poor performance. If I make more than nine errors, I need to apologize to my partner for my poor performance.

- Reach the NVZ 100% of the time after a return, before my opponents can hit a 3rd shot.

- Hit attacking fourth shots, with power and depth, aiming at my opponents' shins, rather than their feet. (Hitting the ball in the air from the transition zone is really hard!)

- In dink rallies, "pinch the middle" by moving to the center line when my opponents are off-balance, and then take incoming dinks in the air and attack them. (I'm naturally inclined to grind out dink rallies and outlast the other team; but that's not the smartest strategy.)

- Maintain a "broad focus of attention" on the positions, balance, and preparation of everyone on the court. (I need to overcome my habit of focusing narrowly on just watching the ball.) A broad focus helps maintain "mindfulness" on the court. (Note: focus of attention and concentration are the subjects of the next Chapter.)

In the section above, I suggested that you prepare a list of areas for your improvement. The list should have at most four or five items. Reviewing your list, what are the critical 20% of the aspects of your game that you need to address? Focusing on the 20% will help you make incremental improvements in key areas. As you improve in these few areas, you will experience qualitative, level-jumping improvements in your play.

Life Lesson

Just as in pickleball, there may be areas in your life where your performance or capabilities have reached a certain plateau and have not developed further. These might include your job skills, career, academic qualifications, friendships, marriage, romantic relationships, hobbies, music, sports, or volunteer activities. We may not personally know or have the opportunity to observe high performers in these activities, and so we may remain unaware of the possibilities for making improvements or even how to get started.

In remaining at plateau levels of performance, we may be experiencing cognitive biases such as WYSIATI, thinking that "what we see is all there is" to our life and relationships. Our System 2 conscious awareness may have been too effective at conserving energy (being lazy) to pursue finding out more. Our System 1 unconscious autopilot may be feeling safe and content with our current performance levels. Due to Selective Attention bias we may see only what we expect to see and overlook the creative possibilities around us.

In considering your life, there may be areas where you haven't yet achieved your "heart's desire." Are there areas where you truly want to improve or expand your capabilities and skills? If you can become aware of these areas, you can consciously overcome the cognitive biases and mental inertia, and you can begin to widen your perspective in preparation for the next big step.

Chapter Five

Improving Focus and Concentration

The previous chapters have addressed several issues that can prevent you from moving up to the next skill level: 1) insufficient time and effort spent on practicing (Chapter 2), 2) lack of immediate and accurate performance feedback (Chapter 3), and 3) not knowing the specific skills and strategies needed for the next level of play (Chapter 4). This chapter discusses another issue holding many players back: insufficient concentration and focus during play. Just as there were cognitive biases and brain performance factors contributing to insufficient practice, feedback, and skill knowledge, there are comparable factors that contribute to inadequate focus while playing.

The cognitive demands of pickleball

Playing pickleball requires a high level of mental performance. The following are some of the mentally challenging aspects of the game.

- **Strategic Thinking** is needed to constantly analyze the game situation and make quick, deliberate decisions about shot selection, positioning, and tactics. Players must anticipate their opponents' moves and adapt their strategy accordingly.

- **Focus and Concentration** are crucial to maintaining intense awareness during points throughout a match, especially during long rallies or high-pressure points. Players need to block out distractions and stay mentally present in the game. One especially important aspect of focus is the ability to see the ball throughout each rally, from the time the ball leaves the opponent's paddle until it reaches your own paddle.

- **Mental Agility** is needed for the fast-paced nature of pickleball, quick decision-making, and adaptability. Players must rapidly process information about ball trajectory, opponent positioning, and court dynamics.

- **Emotional Control** refers to the players' need to manage their emotions, especially after losing points or during stressful situations, in order to maintain a desired level of performance. Players need to cultivate mental toughness in order to overcome setbacks and stay positive.

- **Visualization and Pre-point Routines** are visualization techniques used to mentally practice shots and techniques and to manage stress by visualizing successful outcomes. High-level players develop and use pre-point routines to help maintain focus and prepare mentally for each point.

- **Memory and Pattern Recognition** help players assess their opponents' tendencies, strengths, and weaknesses and adjust their game in real time to play strategically.

- **Spatial Awareness** helps players maintain awareness of their own optimal position on the court, their partner's position (in doubles), and their opponents' positions for effective shot placement and court coverage.

- **Problem-Solving** helps in adapting to different playing styles, court conditions, or unexpected situations, all of which require ongoing problem-solving skills.

- **Communication,** both verbal and non-verbal, is essential (in doubles) for effectively coordinating shots and strategies with a partner during a game. It demands cognitive resources and social awareness. Some players even communicate with hand signals that prompt their partner to expect the next move or to take specific actions or shots.

Competitive pickleball is very much a mental game that requires players to engage in complex thought processes while simultaneously performing demanding physical actions. The ability to manage these mental aspects distinguishes high-quality play from mediocre play.

Consequences of poor concentration

The primary consequence of poor concentration is making too many mistakes, in particular, unforced errors. Even at the professional level, about 75% of points end in an error rather than in a non-returnable shot. In general, unforced errors are due to lapses in concentration (Johnson, 2018). Johnson defines unforced errors as "mistakes made on an easy shot in a non-pressure situation." Certainly, poor technique, bad footwork, and other technical issues can contribute to making errors, but these issues can themselves be a symptom of a lack of focus. If you're not concentrating, you may get off balance and use poor footwork. If you're not concentrating, you may use a poor volley or stroke technique.

The single best way to lift your game immediately is to reduce your error rate. Since lack of concentration is a primary reason for unforced errors, the implication is that ***the single best way to improve your game immediately is through better concentration and focus***!

Certainly, a few errors are to be expected. I recall seeing an interview with professional pickleball player Zane Navratil in which he said his goal is not to be error-free, as that would force him into a conservative, boring playing style. His goal is to minimize unnecessary errors.

As I suggested in Chapter 3, it makes good sense to aim for four or fewer errors per game. In the interest of good feedback, I recommend you count your errors for every game. Unforced errors are shots you would normally hit in, but for some reason missed. Four or fewer errors indicates you are playing with good concentration. If it's five to nine errors, try to reset mentally and get your focus back. I recall playing a game when I was feeling nearly exhausted. I made six errors before the score even moved beyond 0-0, which I realized was truly awful. However, with the score at 0-0, I had time to reset, so I slowed down to get my breathing and heart rate down. I focused on keeping the ball in play, and I was able to play much better. By the way, if my play is in the 10+ error range, I apologize to my partner and offer to buy coffee or a snack after the game!

Why it's hard to maintain concentration and focus

As you review the list of pickleball's cognitively demanding tasks, you can see why constant mental focus is so important. Any slip in concentration results in an immediate decline in one or more aspects of your play. If you get distracted and stop thinking strategically, you no longer take advantage of the situation and your opponents' weaknesses. If you stop focusing on the ball, you begin to miss shots that you would normally return. If you lose control over your emotions, you may become anxious or angry and hit wild or inappropriate shots or even make inappropriate comments.

Recall from Chapter 2 that concentration is a function of your System 2 conscious awareness, with all the accompanying shortcomings, such as limited processing ability and inclination to conserve energy by avoiding intense concentration. It is challenging to think strategically, watch the ball's trajectory, anticipate next shot, observe your partner and opponents all at the same time! Additionally, it's challenging to hit your shots properly, which is more a function of System 1 unconscious thinking. However, in a game situation, your System 2 conscious awareness and System 1 unconscious thinking have to work together seamlessly to perform all aspects of the game.

Given the importance of focusing, why don't we stay focused all the time on the pickleball court? Basically, concentration and focus are forms of mental work that expend energy. The energy for mental focus is quite limited and, when it runs out, we lose the ability to focus and exert self-discipline (Baumeister, 1998). When the energy runs out, our System 2 conscious awareness automatically slips into a sort of mental "neutral gear" called the Default Mode Network. We can also slip into Default Mode when we are distracted or simply lose our task focus.

The impacts of Default Mode Network thinking

The Default Mode Network is a very important feature of our thinking that isn't often discussed in sports psychology and needs some further clarification. There will be nearly constant references to the Default Mode from here on in this book. Here are some of its characteristics of Default Mode thinking:

- Mind wandering or daydreaming

- Looking for possible threats or opportunities in the environment

- Imagining the future

- Feeling regret or remorse for events in the past

- Ruminating and getting stuck in recurring patterns of thinking

- Decreased control over emotions

- Increased negativity bias, seeing problems or concerns rather than opportunities

- Association with experiencing depression, anxiety disorders, and ADHD (Attention Deficit Hyperactive Disorder)

- Decreased confidence in skills and abilities and increased awareness of weaknesses and limitations.

The Default Mode is not all negative. Here are some of its beneficial features:

- Identifying real threats in the environment

- Thinking with originality and creativity. A wandering mind or daydreaming can lead to very creative, original thoughts. It can instigate an "epiphany" experience.

- Generating creative ideas which may emerge when walking in nature or while relaxing

- Understanding others and tapping into our intuitions about others' emotions

- Accessing long-term memory.

The Default Mode uses different parts of the brain than the areas that are activated when we are focused on a task, as shown by brain scan research. The parts of the brain used for concentration and decision-making (mainly the frontal cortex), turn off and stop firing in the Default Mode. Unfortunately, these parts exert considerable control over the emotional centers of the brain and that emotional control is diminished in Default Mode. In Default Mode, with the frontal cortex out of action, emotions can surge out of control. On the court, we can become anxious or angry with little provocation.

From an evolutionary or historical point of view, the Default Mode has clear survival value. In this mode, we are searching for danger in the environment and looking for solutions to problems. On the pickleball court, however, the results are not so good. We start worrying about whether we will win or lose, whether we are playing well, whether our opponents are calling lines fairly, etc. Our game performance deteriorates.

When we regain concentration, the brain shifts out of the Default Mode into what is called the Task Positive Network. In the Task Positive Network mode, we are focused on external events, engaged in goal-oriented behaviors, making decisions, choosing strategies, etc., all related to high-level thinking. Our emotional impulses are much more under control in this mode. The Task Positive Network is essentially the brain's "mission control center" during task-focused activities. The Task Positive Mode is essential for performing tasks that demand high levels of cognitive effort and attention; it helps in maintaining focus and executing complex tasks. However, overreliance on the Task Positive Network without adequate rest can lead to stress and burnout. There is definitely a need for balance between the Task Positive Mode and the Default Mode!

Deliberate attention is the key to shifting into Task Positive Mode (Gawdat, 2022). Any time you shift your focus back to the real world, away from internal rumination and worry, you switch off your Default Mode and turn on the Task Positive Mode. Feelings of internal calm, peace, and confidence immediately increase as the frontal cortex kicks into action. Performance on the pickleball court surges upward as well. In short, staying as much as possible in the Task Positive Mode while playing pickleball will have very positive impacts on your performance.

But how do you stay in Task Positive mode if mental energy is a limited resource that can run out? Fortunately, the ability to stay focused can be increased through practice, just as a muscle can become stronger by exercising it. In addition, the Default Mode can be weakened by using it less. Much of the rest of this chapter is devoted to exercises that strengthen the Task Positive Mode and weaken the Default Mode.

Exercises to stay more in a Task Positive Mode, less in a Default Mode

Gawdat (2023) developed an exercise to increase the Task Positive aspect of our thinking and decrease time in Default Mode. His exercise uses the principle of neuroplasticity to develop the brain circuitry associated with deliberate attention and Task Positive Mode. You can follow these steps to increase your ability to function in the Task Positive mode.

1. Set aside five minutes, several times a day, for the exercise.

2. Start by increasing awareness of your surroundings and end any mental rumination in which you are involved. Look around your environment and notice the details.

3. Give your brain a task to do that will keep you in deliberate thinking mode. Examples can include looking for every white or blue object in the room or your surroundings. Recall the last 10 people you met. Count backwards from 200 to 0 by threes. Compute the number of days until Christmas. Work on a crossword puzzle. Simply become more aware of your breathing and heart beating. The options are endless. The goal is to get your brain to accomplish a short, simple task that guarantees you are in Task Positive mode.

4. Repeat the exercise several times a day; repeat for 21 consecutive

days. In Gawdat's experience, if you can do this for 21 days you will experience a huge improvement in your ability to stay in Task Positive Mode and avoid Default Mode.

Using mindfulness meditation

You may have noticed that Gawdat was actually introducing a form of mindfulness meditation in his exercise, without calling it that. Several writers have specifically recommended mindfulness practice as a way of staying in Task Positive Mode (e.g., Kirchner, 2017; Orman, 2024). Not everyone is interested in meditation per se, but I want to point out that the practice of mindfulness (spiritual or religious issues aside) trains our brain through neuroplasticity to stay engaged in the Task Positive mode and out of the Default Mode. There are many additional benefits to this practice, including reduced feelings of stress and anxiety, feeling more at peace, and being more open to the world around you.

Mindfulness meditation can be done *formally*, in a seated position for a period of time, or *informally* while engaged in other activities. There are many books and resources available about formal mindfulness meditation (e.g., Kabat-Zin, 2013) if you are interested. The informal practice is of special relevance here because it can be used while playing or practicing pickleball.

The simplest way to practice mindfulness is to focus on your breathing. This is often the approach used in formal meditation but can also be used informally. You simply pay close attention to your breathing. You can focus your nostrils, for example, feeling the breath as it flows in and out of your nose. You can focus on your chest, feeling your chest expanding and contracting with each breath. You can also focus on your belly, which also moves in and out with your breath. In each case, you are only aware of your breathing and the feelings associated with it.

Practicing Task Positive Network / Mindfulness between points

One way to maximize the benefits of the Task Positive Network is to practice mindfulness after the completion of each point or rally. At point completion, become aware of your breath flowing in and out of your nostrils, chest, or belly. (I like to use the chest because if I'm breathing hard and gasping for air, the air isn't going through my nostrils.) I also like to count inhales/exhales, going from one to five, then starting over with "one." I try to get in five breaths, at least, before the next point. While noticing my breathing, I look around the court and see the other players, I see my paddle and the ball, I see the court and the surroundings. I take my time, not rushing to get into the next point until I have counted to five.

Right after the point is over is a critical time in the game. The high level of focus required during the point is over. Your brain needs to shift gears a bit and relax from the intense concentration. At this point, you can easily shift out of Task Positive back into Default Mode, especially if you are fatigued. Shifting into calm awareness of your breathing allows your mental energy to recharge while remaining in Task Positive Mode.

Incorporating Task Positive Mode / Mindfulness into your game

One of my favorite tennis writers, Timothy Gallwey (1997), suggests using mindfulness practices based on various sensory modalities in your play and practice sessions. I have used them extensively in tennis since first reading about them in 1974 and have continued using them since switching to pickleball in 2017. His mindfulness practices incorporate vision, sound, and feelings.

Vision. Most people have a hard time seeing the ball well. In fact, I think most people don't know what that statement even means! He suggests the following exercises:

1. See the ball from the time it leaves the opponent's paddle until it reaches your own paddle.

2. See the holes in the ball as it spins toward you.

3. See a corner of the ball, i.e., don't just "see the ball" as you hit it; try to hit a spot on the lower inside or outside corner of the ball.

4. Observe the trajectory of the ball for both your shots and your opponent's shots. Note the height at which it passes over the net, ball speed, angle, etc.

5. See the ball in an effortless, relaxed manner, rather than forcing yourself to stare at it.

You can either do the exercises individually or do all of them at the same time, which is truly great! Using all five exercises at the same time is a "master exercise" for seeing the ball effectively. I practice these as a single exercise regularly during games and during drilling sessions as well.

Sound. The sounds you hear and speak in a game provide useful information about when the ball is hit, how hard, and its spin. Here are exercises for using sound as a form of mindfulness:

- Listen to the sound of the ball as it hits the paddle. Learn to distinguish the sound of topspin versus backspin and solid versus off-center shots.

- Listen to the sound of your own dinks, drives, volleys, overheads, etc. Hitting at the right moment with correct technique and footwork will produce a unique sound. Try to reproduce the sounds of good, solid shots. This is especially useful in hitting a consistent, solid volley.

Vision and Sound. Another exercise Gallwey recommends is called the "bounce-hit" drill, which incorporates both sound and vision aspects of mindfulness. During practice or a game, as you are about to hit the ball, mentally or audibly say "bounce" right when it bounces. Then, as the ball hits your paddle, say "hit," and listen to the sound of the ball bouncing and as it hits your paddle. In a drill, this exercise focuses your mind and helps you maintain concentration for long periods of time. In a game, you automatically both see and hear the ball with focused concentration. (A cautionary note, if you say bounce-hit out loud, people may laugh at you.)

One immediate benefit is a significant improvement in your timing. Somehow, the drill helps create a brief pause right before you hit the ball, where your feet are in place and your body is balanced and stable. This is the essence of good timing on a shot. I've used this drill regularly (in tennis and pickleball) since about 1974; I still use it nearly every time I play. If a friend or practice partner is struggling with their timing or with frequent mishits, I recommend this drill. When they try it, their shots improve immediately. However, this must seem like a silly thing to do, because almost no one remembers to use the drill when they are struggling again at a later time. If I remind them to try the "bounce hit" drill, a frequent response is, "Oh, yeah, I forgot all about that!"

Feel. The feel of the ball hitting the paddle provides useful feedback about how well and how hard the ball was hit and the type and amount of spin. Try the following exercise for the mindfulness of feeling.

- Feel the position of your paddle in your hand as you strike the ball. Even a slight variation in paddle position will have a huge effect on the trajectory of the shot.

- Feel the position of your paddle between shots. Is it centered, in ready position?

- Feel the height of your paddle to ensure it is correctly positioned for your next shot. Use the "seesaw" model for correct paddle position. If your opponent has a high ball, hitting down, move your paddle low, near the ground. If the opponent's paddle is low, the ball will likely come in high, so raise your paddle higher.

- Feel your body during practice. Feel your hand and arm as you swing.

- Feel your legs and feet as you move between shots. Are you fluid and mobile?

- Feel the placement of your feet as you hit your shots. Are you ready and balanced for each new shot? Do you stop and "split step" as your opponent is about to hit the ball?

- Feel the rhythm of your strokes. Every shot has its own natural rhythm. Be aware of the different rhythms of your shots.

- Feel the paddle as the ball impacts it. How do the vibrations feel in a good shot? A bad shot? Remember how a good shot feels and try to replicate that feeling in subsequent shots.

- Feel the state of your body as you move to a shot. Are you tense or relaxed? Focus on relaxing your body feeling calm and ready. Expand your sensory awareness into your whole body.

Improving sensory awareness and focus

Here is an exercise Gallwey suggested to improve sensory awareness and focus. Set up a ball machine on the opposing baseline to hit your hard drives while you are at the NVZ. Practice using all the sensory modalities in hitting your volleys: see the holes in the ball, hit the lower inside corner, hear the sound of your volley and try to duplicate the sound of a solid hit, feel the ball hit the paddle, feel your hands and arms as you hit, feel the location of the paddle between shots. There is a lot to practice!

As you get more comfortable with the pace of the ball, move the ball machine well into the transition zone and repeat the process. Now you have very little time to prepare! Try to return all the balls, even those you normally believe are too fast for you. Stay relaxed. Concentration slows the ball down!

Gallwey used the ball machine drill to speed up his reaction times on tennis serve returns. He was eventually able to stand one foot behind the service line and return even blistering serves with consistency. His location let him get to the net ahead of the server, completely throwing off their timing. Likewise, when we use this drill, we will be able to return even hard-hit volleys and overheads, making us formidable defensive players!

We may not have ready access to a ball machine, but practicing against a wall allows a close approximation. After your normal workout hitting against a wall, move closer and closer to the wall as you hit volleys and drives. Gradually move past your comfort zone until you can barely get the ball back. See the holes in the ball, see a spot on the ball, hear the sound of your shots, feel your hand and arm as you make the shots, feel your body position. Improve your ability to play in such a challenging situation!

Awareness and focus of attention

These sensory exercises help maintain a present moment, Task Positive Network focus, while you play. If you get distracted by mental judgments about your play, remembering all your errors, or worrying about whether you will win or lose (Default Mode thinking), your performance will immediately deteriorate. Present moment awareness leads to "being in the zone" and playing your best. You can focus your awareness on any aspect of your game, as well as your breathing or any of the various sensory modalities (sight, hearing, feeling). Your focus of attention can be very narrow, as in seeing the holes in the ball or trying to hit a particular spot on the ball. Alternatively, your focus can be broad, encompassing the entire court and all the players.

I've seen several videos of top players discussing their focus of attention during a point. These players, as well as nationally known coach Kyle McKenzie, and my own coach Carney Lucas have stressed the importance of keeping a broad focus of attention. The broad focus reveals player positions, their footwork and balance (are they prepared for the next shot or caught off-balance?) and where the attacking opportunities are. The narrow focus tells you the position of your paddle, your footwork, the location of the ball- information about yourself.

Can you keep a narrow and broad focus at the same time? My suspicion is that, just as you cannot be in Task Positive and Default Mode at the same time, you cannot have both a narrow and broad focus at the same time. Other writers agree with this (e.g., Nideffer and Sagal, 2006; Weinberg and Gould, 1995). I think you need to find a way to alternate between a broad and a narrow focus. For example, when you are not hitting the ball, you can maintain a broad focus and be aware of the positions of the other players, whether they are balanced or not, and where attacking opportunities can be found. As the ball approaches you, you can do a split-step, ensure you are in a ready position, and shift to a narrow focus to see the ball clearly as you hit it. After hitting the ball (unless you are in a firefight at the net), you can return to ready position and shift back to the broader focus. The ready position can be a signal to shift your focus.

Attitudes while using mindfulness

There are certain attitudes that are very helpful while engaging in mindfulness exercises during or between points. Jon Kabat-Zin recommends that you maintain the following attitudes in playing pickleball.

1. **Non-judging.** Don't make good or bad evaluations of your play or the play of others during the point. Judgments are associated with Default Mode and lead to a negative spiral.

2. **Patience.** Be patient with yourself and others. If you begin to become upset or agitated by the process of the game (showing Default Mode thinking), return to feeling patience.

3. **Assume a "beginner's mind."** Free yourself of expectations based on previous experience, accept the richness of the present moment.

4. **Trust.** Trust in your skills, abilities, and your own basic wisdom and goodness on the court.

5. **Non-striving.** Allow what is happening to happen. Don't get caught up in self-criticism, feeling like you must win, trying to be in control of the situation (Default Mode thinking).

6. **Acceptance.** See things as they really are; don't engage in resistance or denial of the situation (again, Default Mode actions).

7. **Letting go.** Release negative events or feelings immediately. The previous point is over whether you won or lost it.

Kabat-Zin recommends that we cultivate other states of mind as well to complement these attitudes. These include attitudes of generosity, kindness, gratitude, joy, forgiveness, kindness, empathy, and respect for yourself and others.

Deepening our focus and concentration while playing

The previous section addressed the value of staying in the Task Positive mode and out of the Default Mode of thinking and suggested exercises for maintaining a Task Positive orientation. In this section, I would like to address ways to deepen the ability to concentrate and focus during each point. In the middle of a point, it is very easy to get distracted and not use proper footwork, to forget to watch the ball closely, to forget to use the desired strategy, to overhit the ball, to hit the ball to the wrong location, etc. I have watched many players lose concentration during the progression of a point and make all kinds of errors they normally would not make. This is particularly noticeable when two players are going at each other in a hand battle, or when one team is targeting an opponent with a series of very difficult shots. One person may sustain the exchange for one or two shots, then seemingly give up and miss the next shot. I can almost predict when some players are going to miss the next shot. With better focus, there is no reason we can't keep the ball in play for 10 to 15 shots, or more, if needed.

Concentration exercises

Kam Knight has written a fascinating book called *Concentration* (2023) which is dedicated to improving various aspects of mental focus. He sees concentration as the single most important skill anyone can develop. In his book, he shows how concentration improves our memory, increases creativity, enhances productivity, and even makes our lives safer (e.g., through better driving habits, accident avoidance, awareness of danger). Below are examples of exercises he recommends for improving focus.

Exercise 1: Holding an image

Start in a seated position, relaxed, with your eyes closed. Imagine a simple shape such as a circle, square, or a number. Hold that image in your mind as long as you can. When the image fades, bring it back into focus. When other thoughts intrude, let them go and return to the image. Your mind may be very resistant to this type of concentration, so be patient and return to the image again after again. Repeat the exercise every day, trying to maintain the image for longer periods of time. Spend 10 to 15 minutes per session on the exercise. As you improve on your ability to focus on the image, the ability will transfer to other tasks, including your focus during pickleball games!

Exercise 2: Manipulating images

Sit with your eyes closed, imagine a line and hold that image for a few seconds. Now, do the following manipulations:

1. Imagine seeing the line spin clockwise.

2. Imagine the line reversing direction and spinning counterclockwise.

3. Split the line in two, so you are now seeing two lines.

4. Visualize the lines spinning, but in opposite directions.

5. Split the lines again, so you are seeing four lines. Bring them together to form a square.

6. Picture the square rotating clockwise, then counterclockwise.

7. Turn the image of a square into a three-dimensional box.

8. Imagine each of the six sides of the cube is a different color: orange, yellow, blue, red, green, and white.

9. Imagine the colored cube rotating slowly and horizontally in space, so you can see four sides but not the top and bottom.

10. Rotate the colored cube slowly and vertically, so you can see the top, bottom, and two sides.

If thoughts intrude or you lose the image, let go of the thoughts and return to the image. Conduct the exercise for 10 to 15 minutes.

Exercise 3: Attention to detail

Throughout the day, pay greater attention to details. As you walk down a street, pay attention to the size, shape, style, and color of the houses. Notice the lawns, fences, flowers, and trees. Pay attention to the sounds and smells as well. If you are in a classroom setting, instead of daydreaming, focus closely on what the speaker is saying. If you are shopping, observe details of the stores around you, the people passing by, the sounds, and the smells. Whatever the situation, pay attention to as much detail as possible, letting go of any intrusive thoughts that may appear.

Exercise 4: Pushing the limits of your attention span

Everyone has limits on how long they can focus, but that limit can be greatly expanded with practice. Just as pushing your limits with weights will expand your strength, pushing the limits of your attention will increase your attention span. If you are reading and lose interest, continue reading for an additional chapter. If you are talking with someone and start to lose interest in the conversation, extend the conversation by asking questions or moving to new topics. If you are drilling in pickleball, continue hitting shots for more time than you really want to.

The goal is to engage in mental endurance training. We often decide to stop trying out of habit when we begin to feel a slight boredom or mental discomfort. Here, we are creating a new concentration habit by extending the limits of our attention span.

Exercise 5: Impulse control

Impulse control is an essential life skill (Knight, 2023). In fact, concentration can be seen as a form of impulse control. We are constantly acting on impulses. We feel hungry and get something to eat. We are thirsty and get something to drink. We get bored and move to a new topic. We get annoyed and say something spiteful. While you are writing a report, you may feel a strong impulse to check your email and set the report aside. Impulses can be very powerful, pushing everything else out of awareness until you get what you want. Unfortunately, acting on impulse disrupts concentration. Knight observed that people who have low levels of impulse control are more likely to overeat, procrastinate, overuse drugs and alcohol, and suffer from addictions to various substance. People with high levels of impulse control tend to have healthier relationships and self-esteem. They earn better grades and more money. They suffer less from mental health issues, such as anxiety, depression, and obsessive-compulsive disorder. Through the following exercise, we can boost our impulse awareness, which helps us refrain from responding to impulses and increase the concentration we need to play at our maximum ability.

1. Become aware of the impulse to hit the ball as hard as you can. Reduce the pace on the ball, hit more for control than just power.

2. Be aware of the impulse to go for the line, and instead hit the ball well within the sidelines to deliver a safer shot.

3. Be aware of the impulse to overhit your volleys, especially those that are very low, below the level of the net. Reduce the speed and ensure you get the ball into the court.

4. Be aware of the impulse to go for a very sharp angle shot, which would be brilliant but would have a low probability of success. Go for less angle and make sure the ball goes in.

5. Be aware of other impulses you might experience on the pickleball court. Resist impulses to play too conservatively as well as too aggressively. Resist impulses to criticize your partner for his/her mistakes. Resist impulses to give up when facing difficult opponents.

Resisting impulses is very difficult but an important aspect of improving concentration. Try to be aware of the impulses you experience during the day and practice resisting them, even for a short time. See how long you can resist a strong impulse. Over time you will build a strong habit of not giving in to impulses. Your pickleball game will benefit greatly from the new habit!

Life Lesson

Just like playing pickleball, there are many challenges and opportunities in life that demand our full attention and focus. Most people drift along in Default Mode, daydreaming or ruminating about the past or future. Staying in Default Mode too much of the time has many negative consequences, including tendencies toward procrastination, overly negative thinking, anxiety, and depression. We are far better off spending more time in Task Positive mode. We will be more effective in focusing and completing difficult tasks, we will experience more positive emotions, and we will become more optimistic about life.

We can train ourselves to stay more in Task Positive mode by practicing mindfulness and being more aware of our surroundings. Being able to concentrate and focus are habits just like any form of behavior and can be achieved through intention and practice. We can become more aware of our impulses to act in hasty or thoughtless ways and learn to delay and restrain these impulses. As a result, we can improve our concentration and focus. Developing good impulse control is a huge step toward becoming more effective personally and in our career, relationships, and sports. Here are some things to do outside of the pickleball court to develop impulse control.

1. Become aware of impulses you experience during a conversation. Refrain from impulses to interrupt, to be

sarcastic, to start an argument, to disagree. Pause before responding. If you are shy, resist the impulse to remain silent by speaking up and saying what you want to. Refrain from the impulse to engage in gossip or third-party talk.

2. Be aware of impulses you feel while driving. Refrain from impulses to drive aggressively, rudely, or too fast. If you have an impulse to listen to music, refrain from listening for a short time to work past the impulse.

3. Be aware of impulses you experience when eating. Resist impulses to eat too fast or too much. Pause before eating, chew slowly, do not talk with your mouth full. When you have a strong impulse to order a particular food, or dessert, order something else and skip dessert.

4. When you have an impulse to purchase something, resist the impulse. Wait a period of time before buying it, or do not buy it at all. This is especially relevant when shopping online where it's so easy to make purchases with a click of the mouse.

Overall, we benefit greatly by developing a good balance between the Default Mode (with its potential for rest, mental reset, and creativity) and the Task Positive mode (with its orientation toward present moment awareness, positivity, and mental focus).

Chapter Six

How Limiting Beliefs Affect our Performance

Previous chapters have addressed several strategies needed to move up to the next level. The strategies have included 1) practicing with sufficient time and intensity, 2) seeking immediate performance feedback, 3) learning what skills are needed at the next level, and 4) having sufficient concentration and focus while playing. The next strategy is understanding and correcting the impacts of limiting beliefs on performance.

There are several types of beliefs that are relevant to pickleball performance.

1. **"Empowering beliefs"** provide encouragement and support, pushing us to achieve our potential. These beliefs convey messages that we can do something, for example, "I am capable", "I am always learning and improving," or "I can play at a higher level!"

2. **"Limiting" or "self-defeating" beliefs** create thoughts and feelings of discouragement and doubt, for example, "I'm not

good enough to play at a higher level," "I'm too slow to compete with the good players," or "Pickleball is too competitive for me." These beliefs misleadingly tell us that we <u>can't</u> perform at a certain high level, even though it is actually possible to do so. As will be demonstrated shortly, the underlying, unconscious intent of limiting or self-defeating beliefs is to protect us from risk or harm, however, limiting beliefs actually cause us a great deal of emotional harm and interfere with our athletic performance.

3. **"Contingency beliefs"** suggest that we will be happy or successful when a certain goal is reached, for example, "I will be happy when I reach the 5.0 level" or "I will be satisfied when I can play as well as Brad." As Chris Duncan (2023) points out, we do not become happy or satisfied even when we achieve the desired state. Our state of unhappiness or dissatisfaction is a belief state that remains unchanged. Contingency beliefs keep us from being happy and satisfied in the moment and thus degrade our performance in subtle ways.

Some beliefs are not inherently empowering or limiting. Should we be frugal or freely spend our money? A belief in frugality could be empowering to someone trying to save money, but the belief may be limiting to someone with plenty of money but who can't bear to spend it. Should we try our hardest to rise to the highest possible level in pickleball or be content with our current level? Feeling a need to get to the highest possible level might be empowering to one person, but to someone else it might seem depressing and exhausting. **The focus**

in this chapter will be on beliefs that can readily be identified as either empowering or limiting.

Beliefs as a survival mechanism

Beliefs are ways that we characterize reality as we see it, based on our history of learning and experiences. Beliefs are supposed to reflect the truth and help us perform more effectively in our lives. If we realize a belief is inaccurate (e.g., the world is flat), we can change the belief when we get better data. Beliefs are locked away in the neural networks of the brain, composed of a highly complex network of memories that provide us with a meaning for each situation we encounter (Bayer, 2023).

New situations are always interpreted first through the lens of earlier learning and beliefs. Knowledge from the past helps us interpret new situations quickly and easily, which is crucial in dangerous situations and may even help ensure our survival. In ancient times, when the environment was full of dangers and uncertainty, beliefs about how best to act in different situations were key to survival. For example, if a lion appeared on the trail ahead, having immediate beliefs about what to do informed a life-saving response.

Unfortunately, this type of hard-wired survival mechanism is not necessarily conducive to life in modern times. Due to learned beliefs, we tend to experience each new event in the same way as old events, interpreted through the same old beliefs. As we grow and develop over time, we may learn new information and develop new capabilities, but, for the most part, our beliefs may remain the same. We might have new relationships, but we have the same old beliefs about relationships. Our beliefs shape our perceptions; and, until we can manage and update old beliefs, we are doomed to repeat the same old experiences over and over. We are like Bill Murray in the movie *Groundhog Day*, repeating the same day over and over.

How beliefs affect thoughts, feelings, and actions

In broad terms, beliefs determine our thoughts, thoughts result in emotions, emotions lead to actions, and our actions lead to results of some kind. However, there are two very different pathways, 1) the Positive Belief Pathway to broaden and build responses, and 2) the Limiting Belief Pathway that evokes Fight / Flight / Freeze responses. Each involves very different mental and physiological reactions and leads to entirely different kinds of results. Figure 3 shows how beliefs are related to thoughts, feelings, actions, and results for each pathway.

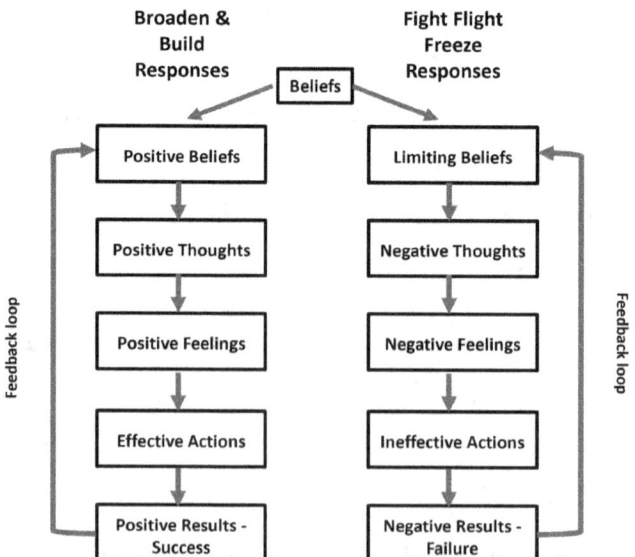

Figure 3. The impact of beliefs on thoughts, feelings, actions, and results

The Positive Belief Pathway

Consider the left-hand Positive Beliefs Pathway (Broaden and Build Responses) first. This side reflects positive beliefs in pickleball skills and abilities and performance while playing. There is an expectation of playing well and having a good chance of winning. These positive beliefs lead to positive thoughts: that our shots will be accurate, that even difficult shots will have a good chance of success, that there is a good chance of winning the game, that our partner will play well, etc. Given these positive beliefs, we feel happy, relaxed, and excited about playing. We are having fun and enjoying playing with our partner. In turn, we play effectively, hitting good shots, anticipating the shots and movement of our partner and opponents, using good strategies, and playing consistently well. The positive result that follows from playing well is either winning or having a great game, full of exciting rallies and an overall pleasant experience. Having these positive results provides feedback that the original positive beliefs were, in fact, appropriate.

The Limiting Belief Pathway

On the right-hand Limiting Beliefs Pathway (Fight, Flight, Freeze Responses), the situation is much different. We may believe that we have weaknesses in our game, aren't as good as the other players, don't believe we can win, don't believe we can play consistently well, and don't believe we are good enough to play with this group. In turn, these beliefs lead to negative thoughts such as "I'm not good enough," "I'm going to make a lot of mistakes," "I'm going to be embarrassed by how badly I play," "The other players will be upset by my poor performance," "I'm not going to win," etc.

These thoughts lead to a broad array of possible negative feelings. These include feeling alarmed, worry, fear, anxiety, stress, embarrassment, or even resentment and anger that we are in an unpleasant situation. Although the game situation isn't life or death, our feelings may be similar to what we would feel in an actual threatening situation. What happens next is that our Default Mode Network will be activated! The Default Mode, always on the alert for danger, may interpret any stressful situation (incorrectly) as one of actual physical danger and react accordingly. It can't tell the difference between a tense pickleball game and a life-or-death physical encounter with an enemy or a wild animal. The negative feelings automatically trigger the Fight / Flight / Freeze response, especially if your emotions are intense. Immediately we will experience a series of physiological responses that impair our ability to play well. These include muscle tension, high heart rate, sudden release of cortisol into the blood stream, shallow breathing, and a shutdown of the brain's cognitive centers so that the ability to think clearly declines significantly. Once the Fight / Flight / Freeze response is triggered, our performance on the court will suffer considerably. We will look and feel stiff and awkward, reflexes will be slowed, shot making will be hampered by the muscle tension and the feelings of shakiness and uncertainty due to the flood of emergency reaction hormones flooding into the blood stream. Because of these physical effects and because we are not thinking clearly, we will make many unforced errors and hit many inappropriate shots. Instead of making four or five unforced errors in a game, we may make 12 or more errors in a single game. Yikes! That's awful! Making so many errors can be even more distressing, leading to a downwards spiral of even more emotional upset and physiological reactions.

As with the Positive Belief Pathway, the results of the Negative Belief Pathway provide feedback regarding the appropriateness of the belief system. Here we thought we would not succeed; indeed, we did not succeed and played badly. Thus, the limiting belief system is confirmed and reinforced. We confirmed the belief that you weren't good enough.

More on the Positive Belief Pathway

Returning to the Positive Belief Pathway, there is a lot more going on than meets the eye. Psychologists and doctors long believed that having positive beliefs and emotions was nice, but only because the Fight / Flight / Freeze reaction wasn't triggered by them. Positive emotions only meant the absence of negative emotions. However, Barbara Fredrickson in her book *Positivity* (2009) described her research on the cognitive and physiological effects of positive thoughts and emotions.

Fredrickson found that, as her research subjects' thoughts and emotions became [drum roll here] more positive (through various experimental manipulations), they experienced additional and unexpected "side effects." They became more creative and better able to solve puzzles and problems (they were smarter!). They could concentrate better, used a broader focus of attention (negative emotions lead to a narrow focus of attention), saw more options in problematic situations, and were better able to cope with adversity. They felt more sociable and open to relationships, exhibited less racial/ethnic bias and stereotyping, and became more willing to help others in need. Additionally, they were more open to the beauty of nature and they were more open to and interested in spiritual or altruistic beliefs.

The improvement in mental functioning associated with positive feelings was astounding. Furthermore, an increase in positive thoughts and emotions resulted in improved physical health, e.g., lower levels of stress hormones, enhanced immune system functioning and resistance to viruses, lower blood pressure, and lower risk of diabetes and stroke. The experience of pain (from illness or injury) was reduced, almost as if the subjects were taking painkillers. Finally, those with more positive thoughts and emotions recovered more quickly from personal crises, such as financial or relationship issues. This is quite a list! It is a list of characteristics and outcomes that all of us would like to have, all of the time!

These findings show that there is actually a physiological counterpart to the Default Mode Network with its Fight / Flight / Freeze physiological responses. This counterpart response operates on the positive emotional pathway. **Fredrickson called this counterpart the "Broaden and Build Effect."** Just as Fight / Flight / Freeze involves certain brain structures and physiological reactions, the Broaden and Build Effect involves quite different brain structures and physiological reactions. The greater the degree of positivity, the greater the Broaden and Build Effect. Fredrickson proposed that Broaden and Build had a historical survival function, in that ancient tribes and communities would behave much differently in a time of plenty and safety than in times of scarcity and danger. During times of plenty, tribal members would be experiencing positive emotions and, as a result, became more intelligent, creative, inventive, and agreeable with others, all from the effects of Broaden and Build. These effects allowed the tribe to build resources, recover from past scarcity, develop new knowledge, and find better ways to hunt and produce food. All were improvements that would enhance their chances of long-term survival. Thus, the Broaden and Build Effect was a perfect complement to the survival mechanism of Fight / Flight / Freeze. Each reaction contributed to survival, just in very different ways and in very different situations.

The implications for us in the realm of pickleball are quite clear. We will play a lot better (and be a lot happier and healthier) on the Broaden and Build track, with its associated positive beliefs, thoughts, feelings, and actions. Several strategies, detailed in Chapter 7, are designed to help us stay on the positive pathway.

The evidence relative to beliefs and athletic performance

Bayer's (2023) model of how beliefs impact performance are supported by considerable research. As suggested by the model, beliefs can have either positive or negative effects on athletic performance. Beauchamp, Kingstone, and Ntoumanis (2023) conducted a meta-analysis of the research literature and found that a belief in performing to the best of your ability has a very positive impact on performance, as does having a strong belief in your own skills and abilities (self-efficacy beliefs). Having these beliefs results in better sports performance and in higher levels of psychological well-being, self-esteem, and motivation. The opposing beliefs (i.e., low performance standards, lack of belief in your abilities) lead to exactly the reverse and decidedly negative outcomes. Similarly, having the belief that "you have to be perfect or others will criticize you," results in poor performance, fear of failure, low motivation, anxiety, depression, and low self-esteem.

How prevalent are positive versus negative self-beliefs in athletes? Several researchers have found that limiting beliefs are quite common in athletes (e.g., Cockerill, 2002; Marlow, 2009). Many of the athletes in these studies were found to hold rigid and extreme beliefs about the importance of winning. Many athletes believed that a loss was a personal failure or that losing would lead to catastrophic outcomes for them. Rigid beliefs about failing resulted in negative and dysfunctional emotions, such as fear and anxiety, which in turn interfered significantly with performance.

Based on these findings and my own experiences over the past seven years, I believe most pickleball players experience some negative and limiting beliefs about their playing skills, abilities, and potential for improvement. There are a lot of beliefs about being too slow, too weak, too old; lacking good hand-eye coordination; lacking endurance, etc. We might believe we have specific weaknesses in our game, such as a terrible forehand, a poor backhand drive, a sloppy volley, an erratic serve, a woeful drop shot, or a pathetic dink. Maybe we believe we're just not cut out for competition, and we don't play well under pressure. We may believe that we don't really have the ability to play at a higher level and we are kidding ourselves to even try.

The origin of limiting beliefs

Where do our negative or limiting pickleball beliefs come from? Christopher Duncan, in his book *You're Not Broken* (2021), describes how limiting beliefs arise from early childhood experiences. As small children we are helpless, powerless, and dependent on others for absolutely everything. Beliefs about being helpless and powerless were quite accurate! Also, as children, we wanted to feel good and experience pain less. Consequently, through trial-and-error experiences, we figured out ways to act that got us what we wanted and stopped (or got very sneaky about) doing things that didn't work or resulted in our being punished. Like rats in a maze, we were rewarded with food and attention for doing "good" things and punished or ignored for doing "bad" things. If we were yelled at for speaking up, we remained silent. If we were rewarded for doing what we were told or for working hard, we soon did what we were told and developed a good work ethic. If there was no reward for working hard, a good work ethic likely did not develop. Duncan pointed out that experiencing pain or punishment was far more impactful on learning than getting a reward. The negativity bias was present even early on in life!

Over the course of several early years, these learning experiences generalized into a set of largely unconscious rules about how we should and should not behave, so as to maximize reward and minimize punishment. In addition, because our brains were not yet fully developed and couldn't accurately identify causes and effects, we took everything personally and believed that we were the cause of everything that happened. That is, if Dad or Mom was upset, we assumed it was because <u>we</u> did something wrong. If we didn't get enough of Dad's or Mom's love, we assumed it was because we weren't good enough to earn it. We believed that not having enough parental love and support was our fault, due to our shortcomings. If we had been good enough, we would have had a full measure of their love. Note that these are very faulty beliefs! The reality, for most of us, was that Dad and Mom had a lot going on in supporting and caring for the family, perhaps they didn't have the time or energy to give us everything we wanted from them, or maybe they were preoccupied with work, chores, health, finances, or other issues. You can see how early childhood experiences can contribute to negative beliefs about ourselves and feelings that we are the cause of the problems around us!

Duncan concluded that nearly everyone creates a set of unwritten beliefs about themselves that include many or all of the following:

- I am not good enough.

- I am not worthy.

- I do not belong.

- I am not perfect.

- I am not capable.

- I am not significant.

Following Duncan's logic, I can see how I developed limiting beliefs that hurt my athletic performance and personal success over the years. For example, growing up, children's opinions were not valued in my family; the adults made all the decisions. You can infer my beliefs about worthiness and personal value! I saw that my dad could repair anything on the car or in our home, with apparent ease, whereas I seemed to have no mechanical ability whatsoever, and I perceived that I was a hindrance on home repair projects. You can guess my beliefs that emerged regarding my intelligence and capability. Also, I had severe asthma as a child and, as a result, was physically weak and lacked endurance for playing sports. It was no big surprise that I was not chosen first for sports teams! You can imagine my beliefs about my athletic ability. Whereas those beliefs may have reflected my reality as a child, they no longer do so. I have, for the most part, corrected these earlier beliefs. Still, vestiges of these beliefs linger in the recesses of my unconscious mind and rise to the surface from time to time. Fortunately, through awareness, the passage of time, maturation, and access to effective tools (to be described in the next chapter), I have been able to convert those limiting beliefs to more empowering ones.

When you reflect on your own family background, can you identify any negative or limiting beliefs? What were the rules in your family? What beliefs did they create in your brain? Think about your own early experiences of failure or not meeting your own expectations or others' expectations. What beliefs about yourself are a result of these experiences? How have they contributed to your own limiting beliefs? ***How are your limiting beliefs adversely affecting your pickleball play to this day?***

A closer look at limiting versus empowering beliefs

In order to help clarify our limiting beliefs, we can consider the work of David Burns, MD, author of the best-selling book W*hen Panic Attacks* (2007), who developed a list of limiting beliefs (he calls them self-defeating beliefs). He developed his list to help his therapy clients recognize negative beliefs and, using one or more of the processes described in his book, convert those beliefs into more realistic and positive ones. Creating more positive beliefs dramatically reduced anxiety, depression, and unhappiness in his patients and had a strong positive impact on their ability to perform better in all aspects of their lives. For us, with athletic performance in mind, our goal is to identify unrealistic and negative beliefs that are interfering with our pickleball performance, change them to more realistic and positive beliefs, and achieve a significant improvement in our ability to play pickleball.

I made some changes to Burn's list to better focus on athletic performance. I rewrote some of the names and definitions for self-defeating beliefs to be less clinical in nature. I added a second column with a term for an empowering belief that complements the self-defeating belief. I also included a new Ability belief category that has more direct relevance for athletic performance. The finalized list of self-defeating and empowering beliefs is provided in Table 3.

There could easily be an additional column in the table labeled "Epiphany," which would be right between the Self-Defeating (limiting) Beliefs and the Empowering (positive) Beliefs. Before we can shift out of a limiting belief into a positive belief, we need to have an epiphany that the limiting belief is wrong. Each limiting belief could be followed by the epiphany, "What the .... that's not right!" We can then be open to the positive belief.

Which of these beliefs apply to you? Think of the implications of any self-defeating beliefs for your pickleball performance. **If you have limiting beliefs in the areas of Perfectionism, Acceptance by Others, Your Worth as a Human, Physical Ability, Intellectual Ability, Potential for Improvement, Need for Approval, and Magical Thinking, your pickleball performance is likely being negatively impacted.** For each negative or limiting belief, all the steps on the Limiting Beliefs track of Bayer's model (presented above) will happen. You will have negative thoughts and negative and unpleasant feelings. You will experience Fight / Flight / Freeze, and you will play below your potential. You will end up with poor results, which confirm in your own mind that the limiting belief was correct.

After you have reviewed the list of self-defeating behaviors, make a list that may apply to you. Think about the impacts these beliefs have on your performance on the pickleball court. Imagine how you might feel and act differently if you were operating from empowering beliefs instead! Include the empowering beliefs on the list. It is very helpful to refer to the empowering beliefs on a regular basis. Your list will be used as data for the next chapter, when the focus is on changing limiting beliefs.

The role of the Default Mode Network in maintaining limiting beliefs

The limiting beliefs that derail our success are maintained and operated by our old friend the Default Mode Network. When we start acting in ways that are outside the boundaries of any of our beliefs, including limiting ones, the Default Mode kicks in and inserts thoughts into our minds to get us to back to the established beliefs. The Default Mode is programmed to assume that our beliefs help ensure our survival, so any actions that are inconsistent with beliefs (limiting or positive) are considered threats to survival.

The thoughts that come from the Default Mode are known more commonly as "self-talk." Self-talk is just your Default Mode talking to you (Gawdat, 2017). For example, if you believe that you are not capable of playing successfully at the next level up, the Default Mode will send you thoughts such as "You can't possibly win a game against the higher-level players." or "You don't belong at that level." It might tell you, "Sign up for the lower level of play." It might create all kinds of thoughts to persuade you that you can't succeed and should withdraw. Negative self-talk is just your Default Mode trying to convince you to stick with your current, tried-and-true belief system.

How is it possible to change beliefs, given the resistance of the Default Mode to any challenge to these beliefs? Change is certainly possible, but it must be done in such a way as to avoid triggering a Default Mode reaction. It is actually very helpful to think of the Default Mode as a person or personality inside your brain trying to help you survive. It is on your side at all times, but it is somewhat obstinate and it thinks in very narrow terms consistent with its current programming. In its desire to keep you safe, it doesn't listen very well to what you want. However, we know for a fact that beliefs can and do change. Think about the beliefs you had as a child and how different they are now, as adults. For example, as a child you probably believed you should not disagree with your parents and had to do whatever they told you. Now as an adult you are relatively free to believe and do whatever you want, within certain legal and cultural limitations.

I was thinking about the tenacity of belief systems last night while watching one of my favorite TV programs called *Longmire*. The series involves a sheriff in a remote county in Wyoming, near a Cheyenne Indian reservation. The tribal members have a very reasonable belief that the Whites are out to get them, a belief that reflects the bad things the Whites did to them over a 100-year period. However, that belief system makes it nearly impossible for them to see that Sheriff Longmire treats them fairly (which he does) or that he regularly arrests Whites who harm tribal members (which he also does). His actions are so contrary to their beliefs, that they essentially cannot even appreciate the sheriff's fair treatment when it is occurring. This is bewildering to Longmire. Further, the previous tribal police chief (the head of law enforcement on the reservation) was corrupt and extorted money from tribal members, so the tribal members came to believe the tribal police would not protect them. The current police chief, however, who was honest and well-intentioned toward the tribe, was also disappointed and bewildered when tribal members treat him with suspicion and mistrust.

Just as learned beliefs understandably blinded the tribal members to the truth in this television series, our own negative self-beliefs can blind us to the truth of our own skills and potential, leading us to discount our talents and successes. I think that many players suffer, perhaps unconsciously, from beliefs that interfere with their ability to play better pickleball and that prevent them from moving to higher levels of play. Think about the experiences of someone who believes they lack the ability to play at the next level. When they walk onto the court with higher-level players, do they feel strong and confident about their upcoming performance? Will they bring their best performance to the game? Or do they doubt their ability to be competitive with their opponents? How will it look if they lose badly? What are their chances of winning? What will the opponents think of them? There can be a lot of self-doubt and troubling self-talk for players, especially at the start of a game. If so, they will be distracted and anxious, and their level of performance will not be at its highest.

Applying life lessons

There are probably many limiting as well as empowering beliefs affecting us adversely and positively in our everyday lives. Review the list of limiting and empowering beliefs provided in Table 2. Which beliefs apply to you? Which empowering beliefs are a part of your belief system? Given the all-pervasive presence of the negativity bias and the way limiting beliefs arise in early childhood (Duncan, 2023), it is likely that you have multiple limiting beliefs.

We have shown in this chapter that limiting beliefs result in negative self-talk and critical thoughts, especially if we try to act in ways inconsistent with these beliefs. We will have negative emotions, and we will feel stressful, anxious, fearful, and depressed. The negative impacts of our limiting beliefs on our physical health can include high blood pressure, high cortisol levels, an impaired immune system, and an enhanced likelihood of diabetes, stroke, or heart problems. Perhaps many health problems currently afflicting our society are due to the ubiquitous nature of limiting beliefs in our population!

On the other hand, the benefits of positive and empowering beliefs are numerous and profound. Acting on positive or empowering beliefs, we experience positive thoughts or, as in the flow state, we experience few or no thoughts at all. We experience the Broaden and Build effects described by Barbara Fredrickson in her research: we become more intelligent, creative, sociable, friendly, open to new experiences, and less biased towards others. We learn more quickly. Life is more productive and enjoyable. Physically, we are less susceptible to illness; we have a lower heart rate and blood pressure; we sleep better, feel less pain, and more readily increase our strength and fitness. We age more slowly and experience fewer of the effects of aging, such as cognitive and physical degeneration. We are healthy and active even in our older years.

Given the two options- Fight / Flight / Freeze or Broaden and Build, the better choice is obvious. We are a lot better off in so many ways if we can operate from positive beliefs and thoughts rather than from self-defeating and limiting beliefs. The next chapter focuses on how to make the change from limiting beliefs to more empowering ones. Spoiler alert, the process involves some reverse engineering of limiting beliefs!

Chapter Seven

Reprogramming Limiting Beliefs

Previous chapters have addressed four strategies needed to move up to the next level. These included 1) practicing with sufficient time and intensity, 2) seeking immediate feedback and tracking performance, 3) learning which skills are needed at the next level, and 4) maintaining sufficient concentration and focus while playing. The previous chapter discussed the adverse effects of limiting or self-defeating beliefs on athletic performance (via Fight / Flight / Freeze reactions), compared to the enhancement effects of positive beliefs, thoughts, and emotions (via Broaden and Build reactions). In this chapter

This chapter provides four specific techniques you can use to create the positive beliefs needed to significantly enhance your ability to play at a higher level:

1. The David Bayer method for reprogramming limiting beliefs

2. The Carol Dweck Fixed versus Growth Mindset approach

3. An approach for reprogramming negative beliefs using self-talk

4. An approach for reprogramming limiting beliefs by disputing their logic.

Approach 1: David Bayer's method for reprogramming limiting beliefs

David Bayer (2023) developed a model showing how beliefs lead to thoughts, which lead to emotions, actions, and outcomes (see Figure 4, which is also the figure provided in Chapter 6 on page 67.) He developed an effective approach to changing limiting beliefs, based on his idea that beliefs are actually decisions made, perhaps unconsciously made, from which thoughts, emotions, and actions follow. We might decide, at an early age and based on biased information, that we have below average physical ability (a limiting belief). The limiting belief leads to negative or self-critical thoughts, which in turn lead to negative emotions, all consistent with the Fight /Flight / Freeze pathway in Figure 4. Bayer refers to this as the low-energy pathway, with lowered cognitive and physical performance.

He developed a strategy for getting out of this pathway and onto the higher energy level, i.e., the Broaden and Build pathway that re-engages the brain's prefrontal cortex and creates a more positive emotional state. The need to get to a higher energy level is consistent with Einstein's famous statement that "We cannot solve our problems with the same level of thinking that created them." To solve a problem, such as reprogramming a limiting belief, we need to elevate our thinking beyond the level in which the problem or limiting belief was created. Given the limited cognitive functioning we experience in Fight / Flight / Freeze mode, the solutions we develop while in this mode won't be nearly as effective as the solutions we develop while in Broaden and Build mode.

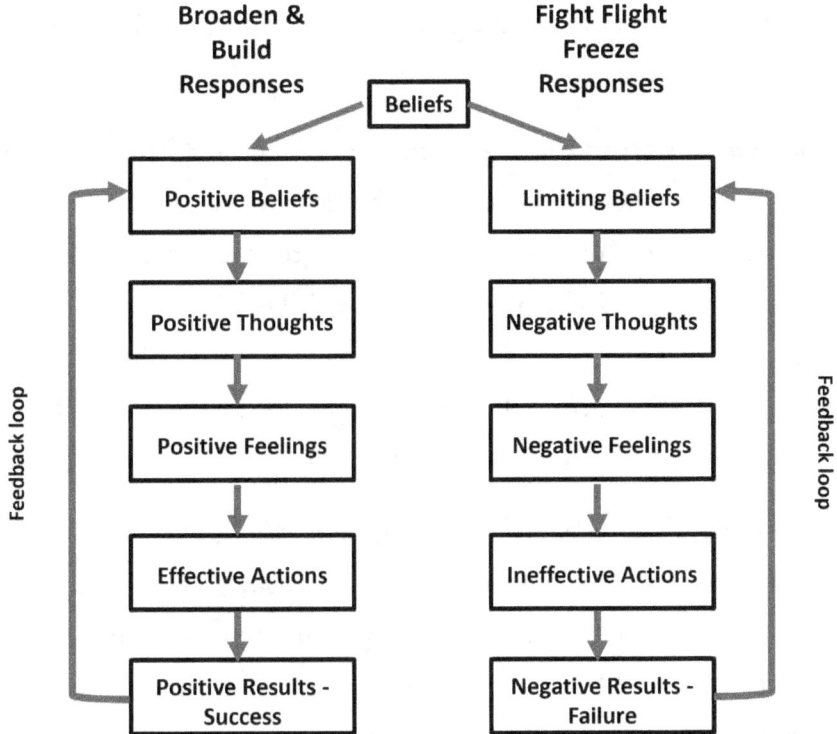

Figure 4. The linkages between beliefs, thoughts, feelings, actions, and results.

The process for changing limiting beliefs

Here are the steps in Bayer's approach for shifting to the Broaden and Build pathway and reprogramming the limiting belief.

Become aware of the limiting belief.

Use this 3-step process to become aware of any limiting beliefs.

a. Begin by noticing how you feel in the moment. Are you experiencing any sort of negative feeling such as stress, worry, or depression? Let's assume you are about to begin a pickleball game with really formidable opponents. You notice you are feeling anxious, stressed, and nervous about the game; this is the Negative Feelings box, right hand pathway in the figure.

b. Back up a step on the figure to look at your thinking. What are your thoughts right now? They might be "I'm not good enough to play with these guys" or "I'll never be able to volley those fast drives of theirs!" or "I'm going to look like an idiot out here!" The negative feelings you are experiencing are caused by some negative thoughts. This is the step where you identify them! This is a shift upwards on the Fight/Flight/Freeze pathway to the Negative Thoughts box.

c. Once you have identified the negative thoughts, ask yourself "What are the beliefs underlying these thoughts?" Answering this question involves another step upward in the model, the negative thoughts must have been caused by some negative beliefs. In this step, you reveal the limiting beliefs causing the negative thoughts. You may have a limiting belief that you're not good enough, you have physical flaws that keep you from playing at a higher level, or that you're not worthy of being a high-level player. Whatever those limiting beliefs might be, now is the time to use the negative thoughts to identify them. This places you in the Limiting Beliefs box, the right-hand pathway.

Make a new decision.

Take these actions to make new decisions by understanding your past experiences and decisions.

a. Realize that the belief you have identified is simply a decision that you made some time in the past. You have unconsciously adopted this belief from your parents or other important people in your life, or from some early life experiences that are no longer relevant. Due to the Confirmation Bias, you have been unconsciously gathering evidence in support of this belief over the years and systematically ignoring any evidence to the contrary. The limiting belief does not reflect the reality of your experiences.

b. With this new understanding, give yourself permission to make a new decision. Be willing to make a new decision. The limiting belief was based on a biased interpretation of your experiences. It is only reasonable to step back and make a new choice.

c. Review the old decision and realize it was really a blessing in disguise because it tells you exactly what you <u>don't</u> want to decide. Reengineer the belief by choosing a belief that is the <u>exact opposite</u> of the limiting belief. If the old belief was "I don't have enough physical ability to play at the next level," the reengineered new belief might be "I <u>absolutely</u> have the physical ability to play at the next level" or "I know I can play at the higher level." If the old belief was "I'm too slow to cover the court," then the reengineered belief might be "I am <u>very</u> capable of moving around the court!" or "I'm fast enough to play at the next level." If the old belief was "I can't improve my backhand," the new belief might be "I <u>can</u> have a great backhand and it's getting better all the time." You are now in the Positive Belief box in the left-hand pathway.

Find evidence that the new decision is true.

Check the validity of your decision by asking questions.

a. Ask yourself, "What evidence is there that the new decision is true?" Then wait patiently for your brain to provide the needed evidence. Bayer notes that your brain is like a search engine. If you ask it for evidence in support of the new belief, it will sort through all of your conscious and unconscious memories and find the needed information. This may take a little time, because you are asking for evidence supporting the opposite of what your brain has normally been seeking. Pay attention to any answers your brain provides. You will remember times when you have shown really good physical ability and were moving around the court with vigor and agility. You will remember hitting many good backhand shots and you will realize how much you have improved over time. You are in the Positive Thoughts box.

b. Ask again: "What evidence is there that the new decision is true?" Wait for more answers to appear. You will receive additional memories or situations supporting the new belief in your capability.

c. Ask a third time: "What evidence is there that the new decision is true?" Wait for additional information to be provided.

d. Begin to see that there is a new reality, in which the new belief is clearly well-supported by the evidence and is, in fact, the truth. With each repetition of the question, you are building momentum toward this new view of reality.

e. As you gain a clear picture of the new, more realistic belief, realize that you had previously adopted the limiting belief based on limited information, and it was never true. Any evidence supporting the limiting belief represented a small minority of the total experiences in your life.

Realizing the benefits of the Broaden and Build pathway

Notice that your energy shifts to a higher level as you begin to gather more evidence in favor of the positive beliefs. You will start to feel more confident and positive. Notice also that the new beliefs feel good and are in complete alignment with what you are trying to create in your life. As you access even more evidence about the new beliefs, you will feel a greater sense of confidence and peace. In addition, you may notice shifts in other related limiting beliefs as they also are converted to a positive form. Your thoughts and feelings will also change in these areas.

Bayer stresses that it is important to be patient with yourself as the changes in beliefs take place. You should be relaxed and curious about the old dormant memories that your brain will bring to the surface as you ask the questions about supporting evidence. The changes to your limiting beliefs may take some time to become firmly entrenched in your brain. You have been searching for evidence supporting the limiting beliefs for a long time, your brain will need a little time to shift to looking for evidence supporting the opposite beliefs. As you become more accustomed to seeing evidence for the new, positive beliefs, you won't attend to the old evidence for the limiting beliefs. Gradually, those neural pathways will dissolve through lack of use, a process known as "neural pruning."

Although the new beliefs may feel a little awkward at first, if you are willing to try this process and give it some time, you will see a huge shift in your beliefs and your thoughts and feelings as well. Your actions will follow, as shown by the model, and you will see significant improvements in your performance! Just imagine how it will feel to shift from feeling that you're not good enough to play with some of the better players, to believing that you are fully capable of playing with them; and then do just that!

Your performance will always be <u>much better</u> when you are operating on the Broaden and Build pathway, when you are experiencing positive emotions, than if you are operating from the limiting beliefs pathway (Fight / Flight / Freeze). Recall Barbara Fredrickson's (2009) research showing that shifting to positive emotions triggered significantly better performance in many areas: intelligence, creativity, strength, and reaction time - all of which are key to improving your pickleball playing ability.

So, when starting a pickleball game, it is important to be in a positive emotional state. How do you do this? Bayer contends that t*he best strategy for having positive feelings is to feel grateful for where you are right now*. Both Bayer and Fredrickson mentioned feeling gratitude as a very effective tactic for shifting your feeling state. You cannot feel gratitude and fear at the same time! You can feel grateful for how much you have improved over the past few months, or since you started playing. You can feel grateful for the beautiful weather, your indoor facility, your new paddle, or feeling well. You need to think grateful thoughts in order for grateful feelings to follow. The idea of feeling grateful for your current state, rather than focusing on how much room there is for improvement, is a key to successfully following this program.

The brain as a search engine

The concept of using your brain as a search engine was introduced in the step of asking for evidence supporting the new empowering belief.

Bayer expanded on this step in his book by describing how to use the brain in an intentional way to answer important questions. When you ask your brain a question, it will search for answers within the databases of the conscious and unconscious mind. Most of us don't use this function of mind (I had no idea that this would work until I read Bayer's commentary). Actually, we use it very ineffectively by asking the wrong questions e.g., why do I always lose to the higher-level players, why is my backhand so weak, why can't I return smashes the way the 4.5-level players do, why can't I move up to the next level? These are all low-energy, Fight / Flight / Freeze pathway types of questions. Your brain will do its best to come up with some answers, but, given the negative wording and coming from the low energy pathway, the answers won't be very helpful.

A much better approach is to ask your brain questions from a positive emotional state on the Broaden and Build pathway. Once you are in a positive emotional state, for example being grateful for who you are and what you have in your life, you can ask, "What is the next step for me to improve my game?" or "How can I get better feedback about my strokes and strategy?" or "How can I significantly improve my consistency and reduce unforced errors?" Your brain will provide answers to these questions once you ask them and give it time to assemble the answers.

Bayer's personal view is that the answers to these questions come not just from our brains, but from a higher source. He believes that a Higher Power (God, the Universe, our higher selves, the collective unconscious) answers us from its position of all-knowing wisdom. Not all of you will feel comfortable going along with that particular spiritual belief, but for those of you who have a faith background, consider where your answers may come from. You might be open to the possibility that your answers are coming from outside yourself, from a source of higher wisdom. If so, you would be wise to listen carefully and act on the answers you receive.

Regardless of your belief system, asking questions of your brain and listening for the answers is an effective and yet underutilized approach for achieving improvement in any area of life. I have made it part of my routine when I'm getting ready for bed at night. I ask a few questions of my brain about next steps and further directions in my life. I listen for any answers in the morning when I wake up.

Approach 2: Carol Dweck's Fixed versus Growth Mindset approach

There is a certain category of limiting beliefs in which we believe that one or more of our abilities are determined at birth due to our genetics and/or the environment, and we are just stuck with them. We might believe we have a certain IQ that determines our intelligence, or a certain level of physical capability that determines how well we can perform at sports, or a certain reaction time that determines how well we can volley or return smashes in pickleball.

This type of limiting belief could be handled by Bayer's three-step process, by backtracking from on-court negative feelings to negative thoughts, back to the underlying beliefs in a fixed ability level and reprogramming a more growth-oriented belief. However, there is considerable research on the topic of a fixed versus growth mindset, and psychologist Carol Dweck (Dweck, 2009) has developed an effective approach for dealing with fixed ability beliefs. Her approach offers you a second tool for managing limiting beliefs. She calls a belief in fixed ability levels a "fixed mindset" and a belief that abilities can be improved a "growth mindset."

The problematic aspects of a fixed mindset

A fixed mindset is problematic for a number of reasons. First, the belief is scientifically incorrect. None of our abilities is fixed. As we practice any activity, through the process of neuroplasticity and neurogenesis, we develop and strengthen the neural pathways associated with the activity; and, over time, we expand the area in our brain associated with this activity. Current research confirms that even abilities such as intelligence and speed of reflexes can be increased. Intelligence is related to the number and quality of neuronal connections in the brain, and the size of the region of the brain involved in processing information. Gaining knowledge about a particular topic results in increased neuronal connections, greater density of neurons associated with this area, and an expansion of the region of the brain associated with this knowledge (Church, 2023). Through study and practice, we become more intelligent about that topic and general intelligence also increases. Research studies have found gains of up to five or more IQ points per year of college attended (see a meta-analysis by Ritchie and Tucker-Drob, 2018). This doesn't sound like much, but after four years of college, a gain of 20 IQ points is an increase of over one full standard deviation! If your IQ was 110 at the start of college and it increased to 130 at graduation, you have moved from the 75th percentile to the 98th percentile! That's an incredible increase in intelligence! Those changes in intelligence proved to be long-lasting, as well.

There are other problematic aspects to having a fixed mindset. For one thing, a fixed mindset is self-defeating and encourages giving up and accepting the perceived limitations of the status quo. In addition, those with a fixed mindset can be very defensive about their abilities and try to prove their capabilities to themselves and others (Dweck, 2009). Those with a fixed mindset constantly fear and dread failure and the "truth" it might expose to themselves and others. Fear of failure becomes an ongoing, unending part of life. The need to continually prove yourself in the classroom, on the pickleball court, in your career, in relationships- the whole process can be completely consuming (Popova, 2014)! Every situation seems to require confirmation of our intelligence and abilities. In the fixed mindset your thoughts are going to be along the lines of: "Will I succeed or fail?", "Will I look coordinated or awkward?" "Will I be accepted or rejected?" "Am I a winner or a loser?". This is an exhausting way to live your life!

The benefits of a Growth Mindset

A Growth Mindset, according to Dweck, reflects a belief that our abilities are malleable and can be improved through practice and learning. This mindset encourages people to embrace challenges as opportunities for improvement, persist despite setbacks, and see failures as growth opportunities. This mindset is entirely consistent with current research findings about the growth and development of neuronal connections and expansion of brain regions associated with new learning (Church, 2023). Once you realize your ability levels can grow, all you have to do is 1) practice with intention (deliberate practice), 2) get feedback on your performance and suggestions for improving, and 3) create an ongoing success and improvement pathway.

Studies comparing people with fixed versus growth mindsets find many positives associated with the growth mindset. In students, they are more engaged in learning, more able to learn after performing poorly, and more likely to take advanced courses and score higher on standardized tests. Students with a growth mindset are three times more likely to score in the top 20% of national tests, while students with a fixed mindset are four times more likely to score in the bottom 20% (Tao, et.al., 2022). Among athletes, those with a growth mindset are more likely to embrace challenges, accept and learn from setbacks, and show more persistence and challenge-seeking behaviors (Dweck, 2009; Ng, 2018; Burnette, et.al., 2013).

Applying the Fixed verses Growth Mindset approach to pickleball

Here is the process Dweck uses to shift from a fixed to a growth mindset, modified slightly to apply to pickleball,

1. Become aware that you are operating from a fixed mindset in one or more areas of your pickleball game. This could apply to specific skills or to more general capabilities such as reflexes or running speed.

2. Realize that the fixed beliefs are scientifically false, i.e., your skill or performance level can definitely improve with practice or training.

3. Determine to think from a growth mindset as much as possible. Recognize and believe that your current skills and abilities simply reflect your skills at the present time. They can be

improved through learning and practice.

4. Identify any fixed mindset "triggers." These are situations that may trigger thoughts such as "I can't do this," "I'm not good enough," "I'm too old," "I'm too slow," or any negative thoughts that reflect underlying limiting beliefs that have been learned in the past.

5. Practice self-awareness and self-reflection. Identify times when you slip into a fixed mindset and intentionally shift to growth mindset thinking. Notice and appreciate the times when you are operating from a growth mindset. Gradually reduce the amount of time spent in a fixed mindset; increase time spent in a growth mindset.

6. Embrace challenges and effort. Seek out opportunities to try out your skills and abilities, realizing that, as Juncewicz (2020) says, "you need to fail and fail often" in order to succeed. What appears to be a failure in the moment is actually a form of feedback you can use to improve.

Shifting to a growth mindset is a powerful way to address the problem of fixed beliefs. There is considerable research data supporting the value of making this shift. Numerous studies have shown that shifting from a fixed to a growth mindset results in a significant improvement in performance, persistence, and satisfaction with the activity. Dweck's method is stated a little differently than Bayer's but is not at all inconsistent. You might consider trying both approaches as you tackle certain limiting beliefs.

Approach 3: Reprogramming negative beliefs using self-talk

Self-talk refers to statements you say to yourself about your abilities and changes you want to make in your life or beliefs. Self-talk was discussed in the last chapter in association with Default Mode thinking. The Default Mode creates negative self-talk to scare you and persuade you not to engage in "risky" activities. However, you can create your own positive self-talk statements and make them into habits to rewire and strengthen positive beliefs. For example, if you want to change your beliefs about your confidence in your pickleball skills, you can create statements such as "I have very effective pickleball skills and strategies" or "I am very confident in my play on the pickleball court." Your statements can be as simple or creative as you would like.

It may not seem as though repeating positive statements to yourself would have any effect. Perhaps the idea even sounds hokey or like B.S., but it is actually a very powerful approach. Many high performers in sports and other fields make extensive use of self-talk to enhance their beliefs in their skills and abilities (Juncewixz, 2017, Niyal, 2020). From a neuronal point of view, each time you concentrate your attention and make a positive statement, you are strengthening the neuronal connections in the brain associated with this belief. The physiological principle involved is exactly the same as what happens when you say negative things to yourself. You may be currently saying to yourself "I'm just not good enough to compete at this level" or "I don't belong on the court with these guys...." With each repetition of either a positive or a negative statement, you are programming your brain to believe the statement. Therefore, repeat positive statements and avoid repeating the negative ones!

In a broader perspective, all of your beliefs have come about through statements you have repeatedly made to yourself. As a child you may have done poorly in sports and told yourself "I really suck at basketball [or whatever]." Likewise, you may have had negative academic experiences in school and told yourself "I'm just not very smart." With repeated negative statements to yourself, you strengthen and reinforce the negative beliefs about your abilities.

If you experienced success in athletics or academics during school, you could easily say positive things to yourself ("I'm really good at basketball" or "I'm a really good student") and develop corresponding positive beliefs about your abilities. Unfortunately, two factors work against this happening. First, given the huge influence of the Negativity Bias, we focus much more on negative events than on positive ones, and the negative events dominate our thoughts much more than positive events. Second, each single negative event has a much more powerful impact than a single positive event. For example, a few negative comments about you by family members, acquaintances, or teachers when you were young may have created deep-seated, negative beliefs and caused lifelong pain and suffering. A few positive comments, on the other hand, would not have had such long-lasting effects. Negative statements are more powerful than positive ones due to programming in the Default Mode Network, which is always on the lookout for risky or dangerous situations. It is not at all on the lookout for positive events! It interprets critical or negative comments as being a threat to your survival and reacts powerfully to them. It may create indelible memories of an unpleasant situation as well as powerful negative beliefs designed to keep you from ever engaging in a situation like that again. This is why traumatic events in childhood, in which the threat was very real, can have such a long-lasting impact on our well-being.

The self-talk reprogramming process

Because positive statements have a much weaker impact than do negative statements, considerable repetition and focused attention are required for success. With this issue in mind, Knight (2019) designed the following process to re-program beliefs.

- Create a set of eight to 12 positive statements describing a belief you want to adopt.

- Repeat each statement to yourself 10 times, concentrating intently on the meaning of the statement. Visualizing the statement will further increase the impact.

- Move on to the next statement and focus on that statement ten times.

- Continue to repeat all the statements on the list ten times each.

- Repeat this process twice a day for 90 days. (The belief will likely become implanted as a habit before the 90 days are up but perform this exercise using the process for the full 90 days just to be sure.)

OK, this is not an easy process! After a few statements, your mind will start to wander off onto other topics or you may not want to continue the exercise. You might actively dislike the process and think it's a waste of time. Nonetheless, your task is to remain focused on the statements and bring your mind back to the task if it wanders off. The focused concentration of the exercise makes it clear to your mind that this is important work!

Here are examples of self-talk statements that could be used for someone who believes that they aren't capable of playing pickleball at the next level, even though, objectively, they have the necessary skills and potential.

1. I would prefer to play above my current level.

2. I have a good knowledge of the strategies needed at the next level.

3. I enjoy playing with higher-level players.

4. I play very consistently and with patience.

5. I can hit the ball where I am aiming.

6. I have fast reflexes when volleying or in hand battles.

7. I can return everything hit to me.

8. I dink consistently well, with good spin and placement.

9. I have a strong, dependable volley.

10. I can reliably hit a drop shot and get to the NVZ quickly.

11. I naturally fit in with the higher-level players.

12. I belong at the next level.

Feel free to modify these statements to fit your own situation and wording preferences. Reduce the number of statements if you think there are too many. To begin the process, find a quiet place where you won't be interrupted. Close your eyes and take a few deep breaths. Repeat the first statement to yourself ten times, visualizing yourself playing with the skills of the higher level and seeing all the improvements you have made over the past few months. Move on to the next statement and repeat it ten times, seeing yourself using effective pickleball strategies as you play. Continue through all the statements. Make the statements confidently, as if they were true right now. Focus on the words, bringing your mind back to them if your attention wanders off.

You may encounter resistance to some statements. You might think "This isn't true" or "This process will never work" or "This is a waste of time." These are all Default Mode attempts to preserve any current limiting beliefs and keep you safe from the risk of failure or discomfort. Recognize the Default Mode-instigated resistance and return to the list. When you are finished with all the statements, open your eyes, and reflect for a moment on the process. See if you can sense a shift in your beliefs towards the beliefs in the statements. Repeat this session later in the day. Continue doing two sessions a day for 90 days. The self-talk exercises will create new neural pathways in your brain that support your positive beliefs and weaken the pathways associated with negative beliefs. On the court, you will find yourself recalling and repeating the positive statements, rather than the negative ones, with a much more positive result!

For other limiting beliefs to be addressed through the self-talk reprogramming process, you will need to draft a set of statements for these beliefs. You might draft statements about your running speed, fast reflexes, ability to anticipate and return your opponent's attacking shots, etc. Fortunately, it's kind of fun to write these statements and not very difficult. For additional examples of programming statements, please refer to Knight's (2023) book *Concentration*.

Using self-talk and visualization to improve skills

The self-talk process is simply a way of creating and strengthening the neuronal connections in your brain to establish desired positive beliefs and thinking patterns. The self-talk process works in much the same way as drilling groundstrokes against a backboard. When you hit many forehands and backhands against the backboard, you're increasing the number and strength of neuronal connections in the brain associated with these actions. Self-talk does the same thing, with hundreds of repetitions of a positive belief statement strengthening neuronal connections and involving the same underlying types of neuronal processes as hundreds of repetitions of a backhand.

On a final note, although it is not <u>necessary</u> to visualize each statement as you make it (using verbal repetition alone is very effective), visualization can make the process <u>even more</u> effective. Visualization strengthens and enhances the impact of repetition on the neuronal connections. In addition, because the same neural pathways are firing during visualization as are used in actual physical situations, you are not only improving your positive beliefs in your skills, you are also improving your <u>actual</u> skills as well. It's a great two-for-one deal, in my opinion.

Knight's self-talk process is quite a bit different from Bayer's approach. Rather than seeking evidence in support of a new belief, this is a sledgehammer-like process to directly reprogram the Default Mode belief system. However, there is no reason that the self-talk approach cannot be used in conjunction with Bayer's approach. In fact, repeating positive belief statements may facilitate finding memories in support of the positive belief.

Approach 4: Reprogramming limiting beliefs by disputing their logic

A fourth approach to changing limiting beliefs is to examine a negative thought or belief, dispute its logic or truthfulness, and reframe the thought or belief into a more logical, realistic, and positive form. The approach described in this section is based on Cognitive Behavior Therapy (CBT) process described by David Burns, MD., in his bestselling book *When Panic Attacks* (2006). The CBT approach is well-researched and has been found to be very effective in changing beliefs as well as treating anxiety disorders, depression, eating disorders, obsessive-compulsive disorder (OCD), substance abuse, and chronic pain and insomnia. Burns claims this approach is more effective at calming strong emotions than prescription medications! Fortunately, CBT has been found to be very effective in a self-help format, as will be used here, without a need for a therapist.

The CBT approach is based on three main assumptions:

1. Beliefs determine thoughts, thoughts determine feelings. (Just as in the Bayer model.)

2. Except in cases of actual physical danger, when you're feeling anxious, stressed, depressed, or experiencing other negative emotions, you are experiencing some form of distorted, illogical

belief or thinking. You are the victim of a "mental con" (Burns, 2006, p. 11). We can identify the con artist as the Default Mode Network, which is trying, in its own strange way, to keep us safe and risk-free.

3. When you change your beliefs and the way you think, particularly when your new thinking is more rational, you will feel a lot better and perform a lot better.

In some ways, the CBT approach is like a growth mindset intervention. With the growth mindset approach, you realize that your fixed beliefs are, in fact, not true. Their falsehood makes it relatively easy to change to the growth mindset. With CBT, we also identify the logical problems or falsehoods associated with limiting beliefs, such as low estimates of our own self-worth or capabilities. As we know, regardless of the falsehood or irrationality of our beliefs, the Default Mode will generate false, irrational, and negative thoughts and emotions to keep us acting in alignment with these beliefs. This is because it doesn't know, or have any way of knowing on its own, which beliefs are rational and which are not. It relies on System 2 Conscious Awareness for input on those issues. Once the Default Mode is made aware that some beliefs are not logical and may, in fact, hurt our chances of survival, it can, indeed it must, change to better support our survival.

Using logic to counter false, irrational, and negative thoughts

So how can logic be used to modify irrational thoughts and Fight / Flight / Freeze physiological reactions produced inappropriately by the

Default Mode? Consider this case: you are hiking in the mountains and realize you are about to step on a venomous snake right in the trail. You immediately freak out, yell, jump backwards, and terrify everyone around you, right? Then you see that it wasn't a snake after all, just a piece of coiled rope. The situation was not dangerous and your initial reaction was understandable but completely inappropriate. You relax, your heart rate slows down, everything is ok within seconds. There is a similar process in CBT - you experience a scary thought, feel an initial surge of alarm, realize that it's just an illogical thought and there is no danger, reframe the thought in more logical terms, and let the initial reaction go and return to normal.

In order to categorize a belief or thought as illogical, some handy categories of illogical thinking are necessary. Below are some terms that were developed by Burns (2006) as the main types of illogical thinking, which he calls "cognitive distortions." They include the following.

1. **All-or-nothing thinking**. You see things in black and white terms. If you're not a complete success at something, you are a total failure.

2. **Overgeneralization.** You project a single negative event into an all-encompassing pattern of failure. You may lose one time to a lower-level player and tell yourself "This always happens" or "I always lose to weaker players."

3. **Mental filter.** You overlook all the positive aspects of what you've accomplished and focus on the negative. Despite all your strokes and tactics having improved over the past six months, all you notice is your poor backhand dink. (Negativity bias rules.)

4. **Jumping to conclusions.** You quickly draw conclusions that are not supported by the facts. You might conclude "I can't play at the next level" when you have barely started to work on the skills needed at that level or "That player is much better than I am" after you see another player hit one good shot.

5. **Mind reading.** You believe people are judging you harshly and looking down on you for the slightest mistake. For example, "my partner will never forgive me for missing that easy volley!"

6. **Catastrophizing.** You tell yourself something terrible is about to happen, such as "I know I'm going to get killed in that tournament coming up!"

7. **Magnification and minimization.** You blow up your weaknesses until they seem huge and, at the same time, diminish your strengths so they seem miniscule. Example: you discount your great ground strokes, serve, volley, etc. and are completely upset by missing an occasional third shot drop.

8. **Emotional reasoning.** You believe your emotions represent reality. Example: because you feel like the weakest player in the group, you must be the weakest. Just because you feel anxious about competing in a tournament, you must be a weak competitor.

9. **Labeling.** You generalize from a single flaw or shortcoming to make it your entire identity. For example, you miss a few backhands, so you categorize yourself as an inconsistent player.

10. **Blame.** Instead of identifying the actual causes of a problem

(which may be complex), you blame yourself when you aren't responsible or you blame others even when they weren't responsible. Example: "My partner's stupid play made us lose that last game!"

For example, suppose you have a limiting belief, such as "I'm not capable of playing at the next level." This belief does not reflect your actual capabilities, instead, it is a negative and distorted belief about them. Naturally, the thoughts that arise from the limiting beliefs are similarly negative and distorted, as are your feelings. Ultimately, your performance will be undermined by these distortions. However, identifying the cognitive distortions present in your thinking can shine a revealing spotlight on the limiting beliefs. Suppose you realize that the limiting belief is just a case of "Jumping to Conclusions" (#4) and perhaps "All or nothing thinking" (#1). Then you don't have to take the limiting belief seriously. It's like the rope in the path that was scary when it looked like a snake, but on closer examination it is nothing. You can rewrite the belief as "I am definitely capable of playing at the next level" and then you can begin to operate from that belief.

Identifying and correcting limiting beliefs

Here is a systematic process for identifying and correcting limiting beliefs and associated thoughts and feelings.

1. Become aware of a negative belief or a thought you are experiencing.

2. Rate the extent to which you perceive the belief or thought to be true, on a 10-point scale, where 10 means it is absolutely,

completely true and 1 means it is completely false.

3. Review the list of cognitive distortions and see if your thoughts might represent one or more of these distortions. Write down the distortions you identify, as many as might apply. (There is no penalty for wrong answers!)

4. Review your list of cognitive distortions and get an understanding of the various errors that were present in your initial thinking.

5. Re-write the thought so it is more realistic, void of any cognitive distortions, and reflects a positive belief.

6. Give this revised, positive thought a rating (from 1 to 10), reflecting how much you believe it is true. Now return to your rating of the original thought. To what extent do you believe the original thought is true? Note whether your belief in the original thought is substantially lower than before.

Here's an example of how the process might work.

1. Become aware of a negative thought or belief you are experiencing. Suppose the thought is "I can't possibly compete at the next level, I'm too slow and uncoordinated." Note feelings that accompany the thought. They might include anxiety, fear, sadness, or even anger at yourself. Write down the thoughts and accompanying feelings in a notebook. Note: writing down these thoughts and feelings is very important!

2. Rate the extent to which you believe that "I can't compete at

the next level," using a 10-point scale. If, for example, you write down an "8," it indicates that you are very certain you aren't good enough to compete.

3. Review the list of cognitive distortions and see if your thoughts might represent one or more of the distortions. The thought "I can't compete...." might be an example of #3 Mental Filter (you focus on any negatives in your game and overlook the positive), #4 Jumping to Conclusions (you've never really tried to compete at the next level and your hasty conclusion doesn't have any data to back it up), #7 Magnification and Minimization (you magnify your weaknesses, shrink your strengths, and conclude that you can't compete), and #8 Emotional Reasoning (because you don't feel confident about playing at the next level, you must actually be incompetent). Write down the relevant cognitive distortions below your statement of the thought and feelings.

4. Re-write the limiting belief or thought, so that it is more realistic and completely void of any cognitive distortions. The revised thought might read "I might need to get some coaching and practice more often, but I am definitely capable of moving my game to the next level."

5. Rate on a 1 to 10 scale your belief in the revised, rational statement. Then review the original rating of your initial distorted thought. Give that old thought a new rating, based on your current thinking. Is your rating of the distorted thought substantially lower than before, perhaps even at a "1"?

The categories of cognitive distortions may seem a little overwhelming at first, but with just a little practice they become familiar and easy to use. You will be able to quickly identify the logical errors involved in any thought that arises. It can become a game. Categorizing others' thoughts as being irrational or illogical can also be fun, but don't expect anyone else (especially spouses or significant others) to appreciate your cleverness!

It may initially seem doubtful that this process will really work. Just remember that your Default Mode uncritically accepts existing beliefs and must rely on your System 2 Conscious Awareness to accept a change in its programming. Your Default Mode sees the logic and power of your analysis, realizes that there is no risk or threat associated with the new belief, and understands that the irrational belief is actually the real problem. It drops its resistance, perhaps needing a little time to adjust, and accepts the new programming. Usually, when you shift to the positive, realistic thought, the negative emotions associated with the distorted thought or belief dissipate quickly. By the end of the five-step process, the negative emotions will be much weaker or gone entirely. It may take several repetitions of the process, addressing the same limiting belief, before you can expect a more permanent shift in the limiting belief to occur.

Chapter Summary

This chapter has focused on the impact of limiting beliefs on pickleball performance. It has included the pervasiveness of limiting beliefs in athletes, and it has discussed how limiting beliefs arise and become resistant to change. Several approaches to changing beliefs were presented:

- Reprogramming negative beliefs by asking your brain for evidence that supports the opposite, empowering belief.

- Shifting from a fixed to a growth mindset.

- Reprogramming beliefs using self-talk.

- Analyzing the irrational thinking underlying limiting beliefs and reframing the beliefs in more positive and logical terms.

All four approaches have a strong basis in neurological functioning and you can use all these approaches on your own without the aid of a therapist. Except for Bayer's method, the approaches to reprogramming beliefs have a strong empirical basis. I have used all four methods personally and have found them to be very effective. Honestly, I thoroughly enjoy the writings and seminars that come from the developers of all of these programs, and I plan to keep learning more about them and using them in the future.

I see no reason why more than one approach could not be used to address a particularly troublesome belief. For example, one belief that has been referred to throughout the book is "I am not capable of playing at a higher level of pickleball." This limiting belief can be addressed by all four approaches. You can start with using Bayer's method to reengineer the belief and identify a positive one instead, asking your brain for evidence in support of the new belief. You can also use the self-talk reprogramming process, perhaps using the exact pickleball-related belief statements provided earlier in this chapter. This approach will take some time to complete, roughly 90 days total, so persistent effort is required. At the same time, this belief reflects multiple irrational and distorted beliefs (e.g., All or Nothing Thinking, Mental Filter, Jumping to Conclusions, Catastrophizing) so it can be amenable to change using Burns' logic analysis and reframing process. Furthermore, the limiting belief may be based on a fixed belief in a certain level of capability. If so, changing to a Growth Mindset will have an additional, powerful effect. I encourage you to use as many different modalities as possible in addressing your own limiting beliefs!

Life Lesson

We all have limiting beliefs in our life. This chapter addresses the theory underlying limiting beliefs and provides four different approaches that can be used to address issues that are well outside the scope of pickleball. These processes can be used to change limiting beliefs you might have about pickleball as well as other many aspects of your life, including your career success, relationships, communication skills, personality traits, intelligence, potential for continuing your educations, and career development activities.

I often hear people say, "If only I had 'X,' I would be happy" or "When I have achieved 'Y,' I will feel successful." I've read many cases where someone thought they would be happy and secure if they had, say $5 million in investments. They worked super-hard, invested wisely, and spent as little as possible until they reached their $5-million investment goal. They were, of course, unhappy throughout that entire process. Unfortunately, they did nothing to address the underlying negative belief that something was lacking in their life, so achieving that goal didn't make them happy. Nothing will create happiness for these people except changing the belief that they needed more to be happy! Using Bayer's reprogramming approach, self-talk reprogramming, or belief analysis and reframing could shift that belief into something more positive, such as "I'm grateful and happy for everything I have in life."

If you find yourself thinking in similar terms, that if you only had 'X' you'd be happy, it means you aren't happy right now. You won't ever be happy until "X" happens. But that's not true- you won't even be happy when "X" finally happens! I suggest you start some belief change work.

If there are areas in your life where you are feeling a sense of disappointment and failure, take a look at any limiting or negative beliefs that might be contributing to the problem. Remember, negative feelings are a sure sign of the presence of limiting beliefs! Similarly, if you are experiencing high levels of stress and anxiety from work, depression or sadness from life events, or even if you feel you are too much of an introvert to have friends and enjoy life ("If only I were an extrovert, I'd enjoy life"), please take a look internally for the limiting or negative beliefs that are contributing to your situation.

Beliefs arise through a natural process of learning, whether as a young child or as an adult. There is nothing mysterious about them, although realizing that many of your beliefs reside at the unconscious level can be disconcerting. If you want to change any of your current beliefs that are problematic or cause you suffering, try one or more of the approaches described in this chapter and begin the change process.

Chapter Eight

Putting It All Together

The previous chapters have provided a set of strategies for improving your pickleball game and moving up to the next level of play. The strategies have included:

1. Strategy #1: Practice regularly, with intensity

2. Strategy # 2: Obtain feedback and track performance

3. Strategy # 3: Identify and adopt the shots and skills needed for the next level

4. Strategy # 4: Maintain sufficient focus, concentration, and awareness

5. Strategy # 5: Overcome limiting beliefs.

For each strategy, I provided explanations of cognitive processes involved in implementing the strategy as well as a discussion of the cognitive biases and limitations that make it difficult to implement the strategy. This final chapter reviews the strategies and key points. I'm also providing an approach for maintaining your momentum with a positive perspective so you are satisfied with your progress and can avoid being frustrated or overwhelmed by the effort required to reach your goals.

Strategy 1: Practice regularly with intensity

The first strategy discussed in Chapter 2 stressed the importance of practicing regularly, at least once or twice a week. It's very important to avoid the "performance paradox" in which you play a lot of games, but your skills become stagnant or even deteriorate. Playing frequently to develop your skills is only effective in the very early stages of learning a new sport. It is not an effective way to build and advance your skills after you have learned the basics. Chapter 2 provided a graph in which the diagonal line indicated how our energy level declines over time during the practice session, so it's important to work on the most difficult shots or drills first. The graph shows "the Dittmar approach" named after the famed circus performer who developed this practice strategy. You should practice the most difficult skills early in the session, when your energy level is high, and then later in the session, when your energy level is lower due to fatigue, practice the skills you have already learned. Throughout the session you need a serious level of intensity to most efficiently trigger neuroplasticity, i.e., the brain's ability to be changed and shaped by our actions and the environment. Intense practice helps rewire your brain for new skills and habits.

Strategy 2: Obtain feedback and track performance

The second strategy emphasized the benefits of getting immediate and accurate feedback about your performance. Sources for feedback can include input from a coach, mentor, or any objective observer with enough skills to give you meaningful feedback. You may also use a video recording for feedback of your practice session or game. Feedback is an inherent aspect of practice sessions, giving you time to experiment, observe the outcomes, and make necessary adjustments to your shots. During an actual game, there is little opportunity to observe your performance or ask others for their input, therefore, making a video of the game and charting your performance can be helpful. Chapter 3 (page 22) included this Figure 5 which shows the two feedback loops that contribute to learning.

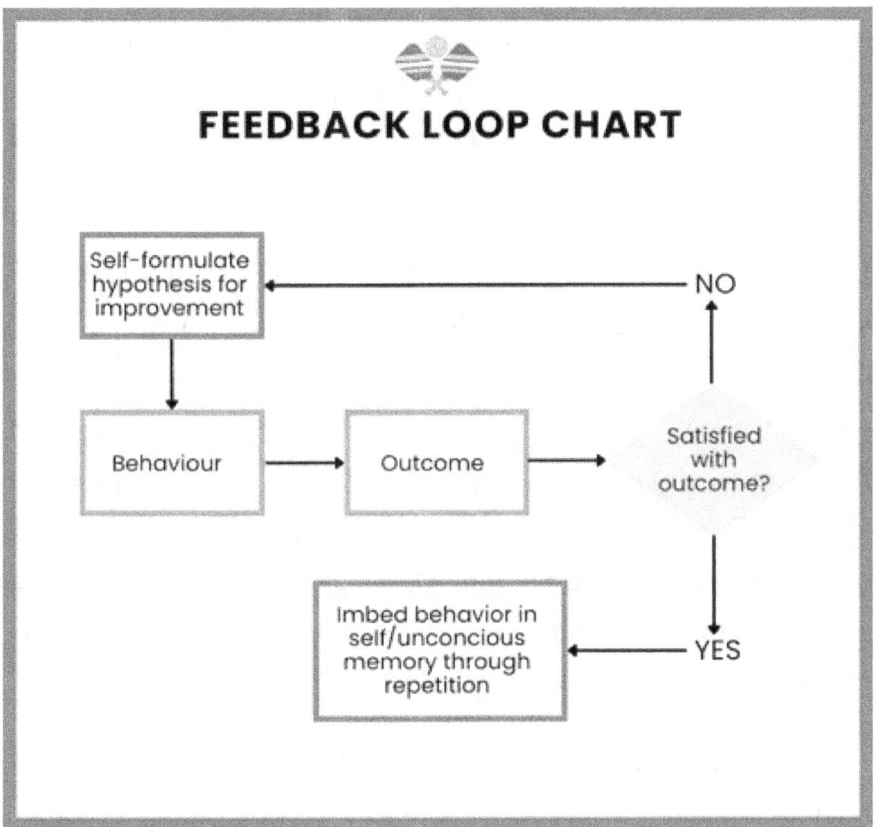

Figure 5. Feedback loops for pickleball skills and strategy development

In one feedback loop involving conscious System 2 Thinking, you work on new skills or strategies first testing out hypotheses related to the mechanics and approaches for implementing them. You might try out a new strategy for hitting your forehand drive, for example, by turning your shoulders and using a smaller swing. Within the feedback loop, you test out this hypothesis ("Behavior" in the figure), observe the result ("Outcome"), and decide whether you have made an improvement ("Satisfied with the Outcome?"). Likely you will need to continue experimenting and tweaking the stroke to really improve it, which may involve many iterations of the upper feedback loop. Eventually, you will be hitting strong forehand drives with great satisfaction in your improved technique. Then you shift to the second feedback loop and imbed the shot in your System 1 Unconscious Thinking through repetition of the shot. You will probably try to improve your forehand from time to time, so, when you do, you can shift back and forth between these two feedback loops.

Unfortunately, we can be reluctant to seek out or listen to feedback due to our cognitive biases which include the Confirmation Bias (we only hear what we want to hear), Egocentric Bias (our own point of view is all that's important), Sunk Cost Fallacy (we don't want to waste all the time we've invested in a given shot, just to start over), and the Dunning-Kruger Effect (as beginners, we have an over-inflated opinion of our expertise). Thus, for improvement, we have to be consciously aware of both the importance of feedback and our unconscious tendency to resist it.

Another important type of feedback is also the simplest: count the number of errors you make and try to reduce them, aiming for four or fewer errors in a game or practice session Many players make 12 to 15 errors per game and are very resistant to being aware of their performance and efforts to improve it. Once you have become conscious of your errors, through awareness and counting, it is fairly easy to significantly reduce the number of errors.

Strategy 3: Identify and adopt shots and skills needed for the next level

Many players are not aware of the shots and strategies needed to play at the next level. They think they just need to improve their current skills in order to move up. However, improving on 3.5-level skills will not develop the effective dinks and drop shots needed at the 4.0 level and higher! Several cognitive biases make it difficult to acknowledge the need for new shots. With Selective Attention, we see only what we expect to see, and we remain unaware of other needed skills such as drop shots and aggressive dinks. In Chapter 4, I discussed another bias, the What You See Is All There Is (WYSIATI) bias, in which we believe that our current level of performance is all there is. With this bias, we falsely conclude that we just have to improve our existing game to move up.

To help increase your awareness of shots and strategies needed to play at the next level, in Chapter 4 I provided a summary of the characteristics for each level of play. The summary includes the shots, skills, and tactics commonly used in pickleball for each graduated level from 2.5 to 5.5+. The characteristics are more completely defined in Appendix B. I recommended that you review the characteristics of the skill level one step higher than your current level of play and identify the new skills and strategies that can help you advance to the next level. I also recommended that you watch Joey Gmuer's "Pickleball Pirates" video series in which he presents common strategies and techniques at each level of play. Instructive and hilarious, his videos provide a productive, entertaining way to identify shots and strategies for each level, which can help you recognize potential needs and shortcomings in your own game.

Strategy 4: Maintain sufficient focus, concentration, and awareness

Pickleball has many challenging cognitive demands, including the needs to 1) focus intently during each point, 2) identify and implement effective strategies against different opponents, 3) remain fully aware of player positions on the court, and 4) control your emotions during the game. Poor concentration results in too many unforced errors and potentially giving away a game that your team had the ability to win. Chapter 5 emphasized that the most effective way to improve your game immediately is to reduce unforced errors, and the best way to accomplish that is to improve your concentration.

When we slip out of the state of concentration that we call the Task Positive Mode, we shift into the Default Mode Network. Unfortunately, in the Default Mode our minds search the environment for dangers and view many aspects of the environment as a threat. Trying to keep us safe, the Default Mode encourages us to avoid taking risks and remain safe. It does so by acting as an internal mental critic that causes us to worry about whether we will win or lose. It fosters doubts about our abilities, and it causes us to experience fear and anxiety. The Default Mode also initiates the physiological Fight / Flight / Freeze response (rapid heart rate, flooding our system with stress hormones, muscle tension, cognitive shutdown) that makes it impossible to perform effectively. All of these thoughts, feelings, and physiological reactions arising from the Default Mode Network interfere strongly with our playing ability.

When we stay focused, in Task Positive Mode, we engage in higher-level thinking, our emotions are under control, and we are able to perform at our best. An effective way to stay in Task Positive Mode is to practice some form of mindfulness. Off the court, this could involve being aware of your surroundings: actively noticing, summarizing, or even counting things around you. On the court, you can focus on your breathing between points, observing air moving in and out of your lungs and counting your breaths. You can count to five, then start over, although you likely won't get past 5 before the next point starts.

Mindful focus on the court also can include seeing the ball all the way to your paddle, seeing the holes in the ball, observing the trajectory and rotation of the ball, and aiming to hit a specific spot on the ball. In Chapter 5 I introduced one of my favorite exercises, the "bounce-hit" drill for use when playing or practicing. I mentally say "bounce" as the ball hits the court and "hit" as the ball reaches my paddle. In my experience, this drill has enormous benefits to your concentration while playing and helps you improve your timing.

In Chapter 5, I also introduced several visualization exercises to help increase your ability to concentrate. In one exercise, you look at a geometric shape (a circle, square, line, etc.), close your eyes, and try to maintain the image as long as possible. (You can use a pickleball instead of a circle, to make it more realistic.) When the image fades, open your eyes, look at the image, and repeat the process. In more advanced versions of the exercise, you can mentally rotate the image in different dimensions and add color as well.

Strategy 5: Overcome limiting beliefs

Beliefs are an important way in which we characterize reality, based on our earlier learning and experiences. New situations are always interpreted through the lens of our beliefs, which help us make decisions quickly and easily about the best course of action. From the perspective of pickleball, we may have learned some negative beliefs about ourselves earlier in life that can hurt our ability to compete or improve. For example, we may believe that we lack the level of skills needed to compete effectively due to our physical shortcomings, that we are unworthy of success, or that we cannot compete at the level of our potential.

Based on the two-column figure (Figure 4 on page 80 in Chapter 6), we act either on the basis of 1) empowering beliefs and the Broaden and Build System or 2) limiting beliefs and the Fight / Flight / Fight system. Limiting beliefs about our skills or abilities ("I'm not good enough") lead to negative thoughts ("I'm going to lose." or "I don't even belong on the court with these guys."), which in turn lead to negative feelings (anxiety and fear) that naturally trigger the Fight / Flight / Freeze response. We then experience the onslaught of many unpleasant reactions: an increased heart rate, muscle tension, sweating, intense negative emotions, the desire to escape, and a significantly reduced ability to think clearly. These reactions lead to ineffective actions on the court including many unforced errors and shots that feel stiff and uncomfortable. Ineffective actions most often lead to bad outcomes, i.e., losing the game, looking bad in front of opponents and observers, and further reducing confidence in our abilities.

The desired pathway is the left-hand pathway in the figure, the Broaden and Build Responses, described by Barbara Fredrickson in her research on the effects of positive emotions. She found that as emotions become more positive, we are more creative and better able to solve problems. In fact, we become more intelligent! We are better able to concentrate; we have a broader focus of attention; we see more options; and we are better able to cope with adversity. We derive a whole array of positive outcomes. The Broaden and Build response is the positive physiological counterpart of the Fight / Flight / Freeze response. If we want to perform up to our potential in pickleball, it is essential that we find ways to maintain positive emotions while we are playing and stay on the Broaden and Build track. Positive or empowering beliefs lead to positive thoughts that in turn lead to positive feelings that trigger the Broaden and Build effect. We have to reprogram limiting beliefs into positive ones in order for the effect to work.

In Chapter 6, I included a table of empowering beliefs that correspond to common self-defeating or limiting beliefs. To maintain your positivity and effectiveness on the court, I recommend that you make it a practice to review these empowering truths (beliefs) from Chapter 6.

- Making mistakes is part of the learning process, to be expected and welcomed.

- People will like me regardless of flaws or mistakes; they may even like me better!

- I am worthy as a human being regardless of my achievements.

- I am strong and healthy, with good reflexes and conditioning, untapped athletic ability and potential.

- I am intelligent and creative and can achieve whatever goals I set for myself.

- My intellectual and physical capabilities are always growing and improving, with vast potential for more growth.

- I am worthy just as I am, regardless of the approval or disapproval of others.

- Happiness and fulfillment come from within, not from the love and approval of others.

- I can be comfortable with who I am, regardless of what others think.

- I can choose to look out for myself, regardless of the expectations or wishes of others.

- I am comfortable expressing my personal beliefs, values, and positions, even if they conflict with others.

Transforming limiting beliefs into empowering beliefs

Chapter 7 addressed reprogramming limiting or self-defeating beliefs into positive or empowering beliefs through four approaches: 1) reengineering negative beliefs, 2) changing from a Fixed to a Growth Mindset, 3) using verbal statements to reprogram beliefs, and 4) challenging the logic and validity of limiting beliefs.

Reengineering negative beliefs

Reprogramming negative beliefs involves backtracking on the Fight / Flight / Freeze pathway from the experience of negative feelings, mentally backtracking to clarify the negative thoughts that trigger these feelings, and mentally backtracking further to identify the limiting or negative beliefs that are the basis for the negative thoughts. Once those beliefs are clarified, you can reengineer the negative beliefs to identify the exact opposite beliefs that are both positive and realistic. Once those positive beliefs are defined, you can use your mind as a search engine to request memories and instances where you experienced those positive beliefs.

As we begin to experience memories of the positive beliefs, thoughts, and feelings, we shift to a positive feeling state, and we jump from the Fight / Flight / Freeze pathway to the Broaden and Build pathway. Your mind can function as a powerful search engine if you ask it the right questions. It can find answers to any questions you ask of it. In this case, you ask to recall memories and instances in which the positive beliefs were true for you. Over time, you can see that the new beliefs are truths, and you can imbed them into your consciousness.

Changing from a Fixed to a Growth Mindset

The second approach, where we have beliefs that our abilities are "fixed" by genetics or the environment, involves shifting to a "Growth Mindset." A Growth Mindset reflects a belief that our abilities are malleable and can be improved through practice and learning. People with a Growth Mindset embrace challenges as opportunities for improvement, they persist despite setbacks, and they see failures as growth opportunities. Once you realize that any and all of your abilities can grow and develop, all you have to do is practice with intention (deliberate practice), get feedback about your performance and how to improve, and create an ongoing success and improvement pathway.

Repetition of verbal statements

The third approach involves directly reprogramming our beliefs through repetition of positive verbal statements. Because positive statements have a much weaker impact than negative statements, considerable repetition and focused attention are required for success. To review, here is the process described in Chapter 7 for reprogramming beliefs.

- Create a set of eight to 12 positive statements describing a belief you want to adopt.

- Repeat each statement to yourself 10 times, concentrating intently on the meaning and relevance. Visualizing the statement increases the impact.

- Move on to the next statement and focus on that statement 10 times.

- Continue to repeat all the statements on the list 10 times each.

- Repeat this process twice a day for 90 days. (The belief will likely become implanted as a habit before the 90 days are up but continue the process for the full 90 days just to be sure.)

The chapter suggested some verbal self-talk statements you can use initially, e.g., I am learning to play at the next higher skill level. I have a good knowledge of the strategies needed at the next level. I enjoy playing with higher-level players. I play very consistently and with patience. The statements can be modified to meet your particular needs.

Identifying the logical flaws of your limiting beliefs

The fourth approach involves identifying the irrational or illogical elements of our limiting beliefs and reframing them in more rational, realistic terms. You might have a limiting belief, such as "I'm not capable of playing at the next level." This belief doesn't reflect your actual capabilities, rather, it is a negative and distorted belief about them. Naturally, the thoughts that arise from such limiting beliefs are similarly negative and distorted, as are your feelings. Ultimately, your performance will be undermined by these distortions. However, identifying the cognitive distortions present in your thinking can shine a revealing spotlight on your limiting beliefs.

Chapter 7 included a set of 10 cognitive distortions. The first five included: 1) All-or-nothing thinking, 2) Overgeneralization, 3) Mental filter, 4) Jumping to conclusions, and 5) Mind reading. Identify which of these distortions you may commonly use and apply this systematic process for rejecting and correcting them.

Next Steps

1. Become aware of a negative belief or a thought you are experiencing.

2. Review the list of cognitive distortions in Chapter 7 to understand how the belief or thought reflects one or more of these distortions.

3. Re-write the thought so that it is more realistic and reflects a positive belief.

4. Keep the new belief in mind, discard the negative belief.

Your pickleball performance will rapidly improve as you incorporate these five strategies:

1. Strategy #1: Practice regularly, with intensity

2. Strategy # 2: Obtain feedback and track performance

3. Strategy # 3: Identify and adopt the shots and skills needed for the next level

4. Strategy # 4: Maintain sufficient focus, concentration, and awareness

5. Strategy # 5: Overcome limiting beliefs.

You will see improvement even if you only use one strategy, such as practicing more. However, adding the other strategies will further amplify your improvement, taking you to a new level. Focus on one strategy at a time but keep all five strategies in mind as you work to improve your game.

I conclude this book with one last suggestion to help you maintain an upbeat, Broaden and Build kind of mood as you implement the strategies. Use the Gain Mindset to focus on how much you have improved, rather than on how much more may be needed to reach your goals. Figure 6 illustrates the Gap Mindset versus the Gain Mindset.

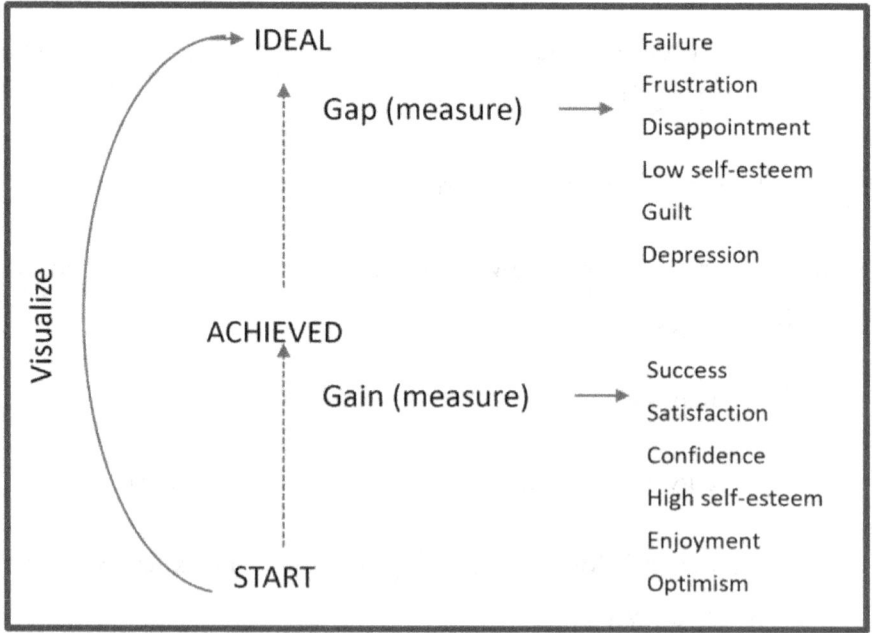

Figure 6. Gap versus Gain Mindset

At the bottom of the figure, "START" refers to the status of your pickleball game 90 days ago. "ACHIEVED" refers to what you have accomplished since the START. The "IDEAL" performance is what you visualize in your mind as the end result of a long time of practice and improvement. Perhaps you are a 4.0-level player and visualize yourself in your ideal state as a 4.5 or 5.0-level player.

Sullivan (2021) explained that if you're comparing your current Achieved performance to your Ideal state, you are in the "Gap Mindset" where you will experience failure, frustration, disappointment, etc., as shown in Figure 6. The Ideal is just too distant to serve as a good point of comparison. In the "Gain Mindset," you compare where you are now with where you were 90 days ago. Look at how much you have accomplished! You are exactly where you need to be at this moment. You still have a way to go to reach your goal at your Ideal level, but you are no longer desperate to get there nor feeling like a failure for not being closer. The Gain Mindset creates freedom and happiness, the Gap Mindset makes you a slave to an unhealthy need.

You can use the Gap versus Gain model to evaluate any aspect of your pickleball game. Have you been working on a two-handed backhand, but aren't quite there yet? If you focus on how far you are from the ideal shot, you will feel frustrated and upset. If, instead, you think about how your two-hander is now much better than it was 90 days ago, you will appreciate your progress and feel a lot better about your game. Sullivan points out that staying in the Gain Mindset will automatically place you in the Broaden and Build pathway of performance discussed in Chapters 6 and 7 of this book. Not only will you <u>feel</u> better, but all aspects of your performance will actually <u>be</u> better.

The Gain Mindset is also a valuable tool to use in your real life, as you aspire to reach important financial, career, relationship, and other goals.

Focusing on what you have gained since you started will be far more productive for implementing improvement strategies than focusing on how long it will take to accomplish your goals. A focus on the Gap is a good way to trigger a life of stress, anxiety, and depression!

I hope you can implement the five strategies we have discussed and maintain a Gain Mindset as you do so. I expect you will see significant improvement in your game! I wrote this book after struggling in my own efforts to play at a higher level, and my goal is to assist others in getting to a higher level of pickleball as well. I am very interested in hearing about your progress and invite you to share updates on your progress and comments on the strategies in this book. I can be reached at joecmont@yahoo.com. I have just a few more closing points to make [phone call in the background]... wait, Phil is on the line and wants me to join him on the courts for some drills. That's it, I'm off to the courts. I wish you the best of luck in raising your game to the next level!

References

Baumeister, R. and Tierney, J. (2012). *Willpower: rediscovering the greatest human strength*. New York: Penguin Books.

Bayer, D. (2023). *A Changed mind: go beyond self-awareness, rewire your brain and reengineer your reality*. Brentwood, TN: Post Hill Press.

Briceno, Eduardo. (2023). *The Performance paradox*. New York: Ballantine Books.

Burnette, J.L., Knouse, L.E., Vavra, D.T., O'Boyle, E., and Brooks, M.A. (2020). Growth mindsets and psychological distress: a meta-analysis. *Clinical Psychology Review*, 77: April.

Burns, D. (2007). *When panic attacks*. New York: Harmony Books.

Church, Dawson. (2020). *Bliss Brain*. Carlsbad, CA: Hay House.

Cornish, Linda (2024). The cognitive benefits of playing pickleball: a smashing good time for your brain. Website: *New Seasons in Life*: Certified Senior Advisors.

Dink Media Team. (2023). *Pickleball 2023 recap: the Dink's biggest takeaways*. www.thedinkpickleball.com

Dittmar, Laido. (2024). *The Art of Practice.* Troutdale, OR: Independent publisher.

Duncan, C. (2021). *You're not broken.* New York: Duncan Publishing.

Dweck, C. (2009). Mindsets: Developing talent through a growth mindset. *Olympic Coaching Magazine*, 21(1), 4-7.

Derickson, Connor. (2023). Pickleball pro life: schedule, workouts and beyond revealed! That pickleball trainer. December.

Ericsson, A. (2016). *Peak: Secrets from the new science of expertise.* New York: Houghton Mifflin, Harcourt.

Fletcher, M. (2019). *Discover mindful eating.* Portland, OR: Skelly Skills

Fogg, B.J. (2020). *Tiny habits.* Boston: Mariner Books Houghton Mifflin.

Fredrickson, Barbara. (2010). *Positivity.* Oxford, England: OneWorld Publications.

Gallwey, W.T. (1997). *The Inner game of tennis.* New York: Random House.

Gawdat, M. (2022). *That little voice in your head: adjust the code that runs your brain.* Bluebird Publishing.

Gingrich, D. and Martin, J. (2024). *Pickleball mindset.* Mindset Publications LLC

Gladwell, Malcolm. (2000). *The Tipping point*: How little things can make a big difference. Little Brown Publishing.

Jha, A. (2021). *Peak mind*. New York: HarperCollins.

Johns, Ben. (2023). *A Day in the life of a pro pickleball athlete*. YouTube video. May 2023.

Juncewicz, B. (2017). *Skilled success*. Troutdale, OR.

Kabat-Zin, J. (2013). *Full catastrophe living: using the wisdom of your body and mind to face stress, pain, and illness.* New York: Bantam Books.

Kahneman, D. (2011). *Thinking fast and slow.* New York: Farrar, Straus and Giroux.

Kirchner, W. (2017). TPN vs. DMN - Neural mechanisms and mindfulness. Website: *Exploring the business brain.*

Khullar, Dhruv. (2023). Burnout, professionalism, and the quality of US health care. *JAMA Health Forum.* 4(3): e230024. Doi:10.1001/jamahealthforum.2023.2024.

Knight, K. (2012). Concentration: maintain laser sharp focus and attention for stretches of five hours or more.

Kwik, J. (2020). *Limitless: upgrade your brain, learn anything faster and unlock your exceptional life.* Carlsbad, CA: Hay House.

Dittmar, Laido. (2024). *The Art of practice: same effort, twice the progress, any skill*. Self-published.

McDaniels, M. (2021). *How our brains betray us.* Self-published.

Maisel, E. and Maisel, A. (2010). *Brainstorm: harnessing the power of productive obsessions.* Novato, CA: New World Publications.

Ng, B. (2018). The Neuroscience of growth mindset and intrinsic motivation. *Brain Science*, 8(2), 1-10.

Orman, R. (2024). Default mode network vs. Task Positive Network: how our brains balance mind wandering and focused attention. Website: Orman Physician Coaching. https://roborman.com/stimulus/119-default-mode-network-vs-task-positive-network-how-our-brains-balance-mind-wandering-and-focused-attention

Perlmutter, D. (2023). Pickleball and your brain. Blog: June 28, 2023.

Robson, D. (2022). *The Expectation effect*. New York: Henry Holt and Company.

Ritchie, S.J. and Tucker-Drob, E.M. (2018). How much does education improve intelligence? *Psychological Science*, 29(8), 1358-1369.

Sayed, Matthew. (2010). *Bounce*. New York: Harper-Collins.

Schneider, V.; Healy, A.; Carlson, K.; Buck-Gengler, C.; and Barshi, I. (2019). How much is remembered as a function of presentation modality? *Memory*. Feb. 27(2). 261-267.

Simmons, D.J. & Chabris, C.F. (1999). Gorillas in our midst: sustained inattentional blindness for dynamic events. *Perception*, 28(9), 1059-1074.

Sodato, N. Okada, T., Honda, M. & Yonekura, Y. (1998). Activation of the primary visual cortex in blind humans during braille reading. *Neuroscience Letters*, 253(2), 115-118.

Sullivan, D. and Hardy, B. (2021). *The gap and the gain*. Carlsbad, CA: Hay House.

Tao, W., Zhao, D., I. Horton, X. Tian, Z. Xu, and H. Sun. (2022). The influence of growth mindset on the mental health and life events of college students. *Frontiers in Psychology,* vol. 13.

Wenger, W. and Poe, R. (1996). *The Einstein factor*. New York: Gramercy Books.

Appendix

Appendix A: Pickleball Game Charting Tool

	Pickleball Game Charting Tool		
Metric #	Statistic Name:	A. Your Team Service Points	B. Your Team Return Points
1	Percent of deep serves/returns (ball lands in rear 25% of court)		
2	3rd Shot drives versus drops (3rd shot drop=1, drive=2)		N/A
3	Your Team Reached NVZ (Y/N) after the return?	N/A	
4	Your Team hit a Non-returnable Shot		
5	Your Team Made an Error (count or code type of error)		
6	Opponents hit a non-returnable shot		
7	Opponents made an error		

Appendix B: Comparisons of Pickleball Skills with the Next Level

Comparison of a 2.0 to a 2.5 player

The key differences between a 2.0 and a 2.5 level pickleball player are:

- Experience and Knowledge:

- 2.5 players have slightly more experience and a better understanding of the basic rules and gameplay.

- 2.0 players are true beginners with minimal knowledge of the game.

- Serving:

- 2.5 players can serve with some consistency, though placement may still be inconsistent.

- 2.0 players are still learning to serve legally and consistently.

- Shot Execution:

- 2.5 players can execute basic shots (forehand, backhand) with more consistency.

- 2.0 players struggle with basic shot execution and consistency.

- Court Positioning:

- 2.5 players have a basic understanding of court positioning and may attempt to move to the non-volley zone.

- 2.0 players often remain at the baseline and have limited court awareness.

- Rallies:

- 2.5 players can sustain short rallies with slower-paced shots.

- 2.0 players typically have very short rallies due to frequent errors.

- Dinking:

- 2.5 players may attempt basic dinking, though with limited control.

- 2.0 players rarely attempt or understand the concept of dinking.

- Strategy:

- 2.5 players begin to understand basic strategy, like playing to an opponent's backhand.

- 2.0 players focus solely on getting the ball over the net with little strategic thought.

- Scoring:

- 2.5 players generally understand the scoring system and can keep score.

- 2.0 players may still struggle with understanding and applying the scoring rules.

In summary, 2.5 players show slightly more consistency, better shot execution, and a deeper understanding of basic gameplay compared to 2.0 players who are still in the very early stages of learning the sport.

Drills to move to the 2.5 level

To help a 2.0 player move up to the 2.5 level in pickleball, focus on these fundamental drills and practice areas:

- Serve Consistency Drill:

- Practice serving from both sides of the court, aiming to get the ball in the correct service box consistently.

- Start with underhand serves and focus on accuracy rather than power.

- Basic Forehand and Backhand Drill:

- Stand at the baseline and have a partner feed you balls.

- Practice hitting forehand and backhand groundstrokes, focusing on getting the ball over the net and in bounds.

- Volley Practice:

- Stand near the kitchen line and have a partner gently toss balls to you.

- Practice hitting soft volleys back, focusing on control rather than power.

- Dinking Introduction:

- Stand at the kitchen line with a partner and practice hitting soft shots back and forth over the net.

- Focus on keeping the ball low and landing it in the kitchen area.

- Return of Serve Drill:

- Have a partner serve to you and practice returning the serve.

- Focus on getting the ball back in play consistently.

- Movement Drill:

- Set up cones on the court and practice moving quickly between them.

- This helps improve footwork and court coverage.

- Wall Practice:

- If you have access to a wall, practice hitting various shots against it to improve hand-eye coordination and consistency.

- Rules and Scoring Practice:

- Spend time learning and practicing the scoring system and basic rules.

- Play practice games focusing on correct scoring and rule application.

- Partner Communication Drill:

- Practice calling "mine" or "yours" with a partner when balls are hit between you.

- This helps develop basic on-court communication.

- Paddle Grip Drill:

- Practice holding the paddle correctly for different shots (continental grip for volleys, eastern for groundstrokes).

- Hit balls against a wall or with a partner, focusing on maintaining the correct grip.

At this level, the focus should be on developing basic consistency, understanding the rules, and enjoying the game. Engage in regular practice and playing with others to gain experience and comfort on the court.

Comparison of a 2.5 to a 3.0 player

The key differences between a 2.5 and a 3.0 level player are:

- Experience and Court Awareness

- 3.0 players have gained more experience and confidence on the court compared to beginners.

- 2.5 players are still learning the basic rules, techniques, and strategies of pickleball.

- Court Coverage and Movement

- 3.0 players have improved court coverage and are more comfortable moving around the pickleball court.

- 2.5 players are still developing their court movement and positioning.

- Serving and Returning

- 3.0 players have more consistent serves, focusing on placement and variety. Some may start experimenting with spin.

- 2.5 players are still working on developing a consistent serve and return.

- Dinking and Volleys

- 3.0 players show improved control and touch in dinking and volleying, though the ball may still sit high.

- 2.5 players are just beginning to understand the concept of dinking and may struggle with control.

- Rallies and Gameplay

- 3.0 players can engage in longer rallies and are more comfortable with fast-paced play.

- 2.5 players typically have shorter rallies and may struggle with pace.

- Strategy

- 3.0 players are starting to develop a better understanding of strategy, including when to be aggressive or defensive.

- 2.5 players are still focused on basic shot execution rather than strategic play.

- Scoring and Rules

- 3.0 players are comfortable with the scoring sequence and staggered start positions.

- 2.5 players may still struggle with understanding and applying the rules consistently.

In summary, 3.0 players demonstrate more consistency, better shot control, and a deeper understanding of the game compared to 2.5 players who are still in the early stages of developing their skills and game knowledge.

Drills to move to the 3.0 level

- The drills that can be used to move from a 2.5 to a 3.0 level include:

- To move from a 2.5 to a 3.0 level in pickleball, focus on these key drills and practice areas:

- Serving and Return Consistency:

- Practice serving to different areas of the service box, aiming for depth and consistency.

- Work on returning serves with control, focusing on getting the ball back in play consistently.

- Dinking Drill:

- Start at the kitchen line with a partner and practice soft dinks back and forth.

- Vary placement between forehand and backhand sides.

- Focus on keeping the ball low and unattackable

- Third Shot Drop Drill:

- Have one player at the baseline and one at the kitchen line.

- Baseline player practices hitting soft drops into the kitchen.

- Kitchen player tries to return the ball deep to keep the baseline player back

- Volley Practice:

- Stand at the kitchen line and have a partner feed you balls to volley.

- Work on both forehand and backhand volleys.

- Focus on control rather than power.

- Groundstroke Consistency:

- Rally with a partner from the baseline, focusing on keeping the ball in play.

- Gradually work on directing your shots to different areas of the court.

- Footwork and Positioning Drill:

- Practice moving quickly to the non-volley zone when opportunities arise.

- Work on proper court positioning in doubles play

- Wall Drills: If you have access to a wall, practice various shots against it to improve consistency and control

- Transition Drill:

- Start at the baseline, have a partner at the net feed you balls, and practice moving forward to the kitchen line.

- This helps with court coverage and movement

The key at this level is to focus on consistency and reducing unforced errors. Aim to keep the ball in play longer and let your opponents make mistakes. As you practice these drills, you'll develop better control, improved shot selection, and a deeper understanding of court positioning, which are all characteristics of a 3.0 player.

Comparison of a 3.0 to a 3.5 player

The key differences between a 3.0 and 3.5 level pickleball player are:

- Serve and Return

- 3.5 players can effectively use their own serving strategies and maintain short rallies. They demonstrate how to serve deep

- 3.0 players are beginning to perfect their serve and understand the different personalities of gameplay

- Rallying and Dinking

- 3.5 players can effectively use the two-bounce rule and catch on to patterns of pickleball gameplay

- 3.0 players move comfortably across the court and can complete successful serves often

- Shot Selection and Control

- 3.5 players demonstrate improved consistency in hitting drops and resets under pressure

- 3.0 players are still in "big swing mode", with too many drives, hardly getting good drops in, and rarely having long dinking rallies

- Awareness of Opponent's Weaknesses

- 3.5 players can recognize an opponent's weakness and exploit it to their advantage

- 3.0 players are beginning to understand the different personalities of gameplay

The main differences are that 3.5 players have better serves, returns, dinking consistency, and strategic awareness to identify and attack opponents' weaknesses. They make fewer unforced errors and have more control over the depth and placement of their shots compared to 3.0 players.

Drills to move to the 3.5 level

Here are some effective drills a 3.0 level pickleball player can use to improve their game and reach the 3.5 level:

- Transition to the Kitchen Drill

- Start at the baseline and have your partner feed you balls. Your goal is to hit as many shots as needed to get to the kitchen line.

- Once at the kitchen, play out the point down the line. Keep score and play games to 7 or 11, then switch roles.

- This drill practices drops from the baseline, resets/drops from midcourt, and dinks at the kitchen - shots that are challenging for 3.0 players but key for 3.5 level

- Dinking Drills

- Play dink games to 7, starting at the kitchen line and dinking cross-court. Focus on keeping dinks low, deep, and consistent

- Drill dinking out of the air to avoid unnecessary movement and stay in position at the non-volley zone.

- Once consistent with flat dinks, work on adding spin to your dinks as a 3.5 player would

- .Backhand Drills

- Develop a reliable two-handed backhand by drilling backhands with a partner. A strong backhand is important against opponents who will attack this side

- Use the proper grip for your backhand to keep the paddle face open or closed as needed.

- Footwork and Positioning Drills

- Drill good kitchen line positioning and footwork. Stay in an athletic stance with knees bent and feet shoulder-width apart. Crab walk side-to-side without crossing feet

- Drill volleys out of the air at the kitchen line to improve taking balls early and staying in position.

The keys are focused practice time, watching higher-level play to learn, and identifying weaknesses to improve. With dedication, the jump from 3.0 to 3.5 is achievable in 6 months to a year for most players.

Comparison of a 3.5 to a 4.0 player

The key differences between a 3.5 and a 4.0 level pickleball player are:

- Consistency: 4.0 players demonstrate improved consistency in their shots compared to 3.5 players

- Control: 4.0 players have better control over their shots, including depth, pace, and placement

- Strategic ability: 4.0 players show more advanced strategic thinking and are more aware of their opponents' strengths and weaknesses

- Shot selection: 4.0 players know when to deploy power shots versus soft shots against their opponents, while 3.5 players may know the difference but lack the tactical awareness of when to use them

- Stroke mechanics: While 3.5 players have improved stroke mechanics, they may still struggle with controlling depth and variability. 4.0 players have better control over these aspects

- Backhand: 3.5 players are still learning backhand mechanics and may avoid it if possible. 4.0 players have better backhand mechanics, but it's still not entirely consistent

- Dinking: 4.0 players can control the height and pace of dinks better than 3.5 players, but they may still end dinking rallies too soon

- Approach to the net: 4.0 players approach the net more strategically compared to 3.5 players

- Adaptability: 4.0 players can shift between low-, medium-, and high-paced shots more easily than 3.5 players

- Overall game: 4.0 players generally have better consistency, control, and strategic capabilities across all aspects of the game compared to 3.5 players

These differences highlight the progression in skills, strategy, and overall game awareness as players move from the 3.5 to the 4.0 level in pickleball.

Drills to move to the 4.0 level

Here are some effective drills a 3.5 level pickleball player can use to improve their game and move up to the 4.0 level:

- Dinking Drills

- Play dink games to 7, with both players starting at the kitchen line and dinking cross-court. Focus on keeping the dinks low, deep, and with minimal errors

- Drill dinking out of the air to avoid unnecessary movement and stay in position at the non-volley zone

- Work on adding spin to your dinks once you can consistently dink flat without missing

- Third Shot Drop Drills

- Instead of always going for perfect, low third shot drops, practice hitting higher, topspin resets to neutralize the point. Aim for consistency over perfection

- Drill third shot drops with a partner, focusing on getting the ball over the net and landing it in the kitchen. Gradually work on lowering the trajectory as you improve

- Reset and Transition Drills

- Practice resetting fast-paced balls by returning them over the net at a slower speed. Focus on soft hands and taking pace off the ball

- Drill reset, speedup, and transition scenarios to ingrain these shots into your game

- Backhand Drills

- Develop a reliable two-handed backhand shot by drilling backhands with a partner. A strong backhand is key against opponents who will attack this side

- Use the proper grip for your backhand to keep the paddle face open or closed as needed

- Footwork and Positioning Drills

- Drill good kitchen line positioning and footwork. Stay in an athletic stance with knees bent and feet shoulder-width apart. Crab walk side-to-side without crossing your feet

- Drill volleys out of the air at the kitchen line to improve your ability to take balls early and stay in position

The keys are putting in focused practice time, watching higher-level play to learn, and having the self-awareness to identify and improve weaknesses in your game. With dedication and smart practice, the jump from 3.5 to 4.0 is very achievable for most players in 6 months to a year.

Comparison of a 4.0 to a 4.5 level player

The main differences between a 4.0 and a 4.5 level pickleball player are:

- Consistency: 4.5 players make fewer unforced errors and are more consistent in their shot execution compared to 4.0 players

- Power and offensive play: 4.5 players can use power more effectively to create offensive situations, while 4.0 players may be consistent but lack the same level of power

- Dinking ability: 4.5 players have better control over dink shots, varying depth and speed to create opportunities. They are more adept at sustaining longer dinking rallies and creating dead dinks to set up attacks

- Shot selection and placement: 4.5 players demonstrate more deliberate and strategic shot selection and placement

- Third shot execution: 4.5 players have mastered various third shot choices and strategies, consistently executing both drop shots and drives from both forehand and backhand sides

- Volleying skills: 4.5 players are more comfortable with advanced volley techniques, including blocking hard volleys, placing overheads, and executing swinging volleys

- Strategy and adaptability: 4.5 players exhibit a higher level of strategic play, working more effectively with their partners and adapting their game plan based on opponents' strengths and weaknesses

- Athleticism and court coverage: 4.5 players generally display better footwork, quicker movement, and more efficient weight transfer, allowing for better court coverage

- Serve and return quality: 4.5 players have developed a higher level of variety, depth, and pace in their serves and returns compared to 4.0 players

- Overall game understanding: 4.5 players have a deeper understanding of the game, including advanced rules, court positioning, and the ability to read opponents more effectively

These differences collectively contribute to a more refined and competitive level of play for 4.5 players compared to their 4.0 counterparts.

Drills to move to the 4.5 level

Here are some key drills that can help a 4.0 player improve to a 4.5 level in pickleball:

- Backhand Reset Drill: Practice consistent backhand resets, focusing on soft grip and proper technique. This is considered a crucial shot for advancing to higher levels

- Reset and Counter Drill: Mix up resets with counters. Practice 2-3 resets in a row, then counter on the third attack. This helps develop variation in shot selection and improves offensive capabilities

- Hot Hands Drill: Stand at the kitchen line while a partner feeds hard pace balls from the baseline, varying left to right. This improves hand speed, reaction time, and volley skills. Start slow and gradually increase pace

- Drive and Drop Alternate Shots Drill: From the baseline, alternate between drive shots and drop shots while your partner feeds balls from the kitchen line. Aim for 10-20 consecutive successful shots. This improves shot selection and execution of both aggressive and soft shots

- Dinking Drills: Practice cross-court and straight dinks on both sides of the court. At higher levels, more time is spent in dinking exchanges, so improving this skill is crucial

- Serve Variety Drill: Practice serving both deep and short, varying from left to right sides. This improves your ability to mix up serves and keep opponents off balance

- Hands Battle Drill: Stand at the kitchen line with a partner and trade volleys, starting slow and gradually increasing speed. This builds hand speed and improves your ability to handle fast exchanges at the net

- Remember, consistent practice of these drills, along with focusing on reducing unforced errors and improving overall game strategy, will help in progressing from a 4.0 to a 4.5 level. Additionally, treating recreational games as opportunities for long-term improvement rather than just focusing on winning can be beneficial for skill development

Comparison of a 4.5 to a 5.0 level player

The main differences between a 4.5 and a 5.0 level pickleball player are:

- Consistency and control: 5.0 players demonstrate significantly higher consistency and control in all aspects of their game compared to 4.5 players

- Serve and return quality: 5.0 players have more aggressive serves with deeper placement, more spin, and better variety. Their returns are also deeper, can be sliced, and keep opponents off balance

- Third and fourth shot execution: 5.0 players excel at third shot drops and drives, and are particularly adept at fourth shot strategies, such as angled backhand blocks to the opponent's feet

- Volleying skills: 5.0 players hit more punishing volleys, often targeting the opponent's inner foot with precision and power

- Dinking ability: While 4.5 players can sustain dinking rallies, 5.0 players make fewer errors in dinking exchanges and are better at creating and capitalizing on offensive opportunities during these rallies

- Offensive dinking: 5.0 players are more proficient at hitting offensive dinks past the kitchen line, putting pressure on their opponents

- Strategic play: 5.0 players demonstrate more advanced strategic thinking, often planning several moves ahead and adapting their game plan more effectively

- Hand speed and anticipation: 5.0 players generally have faster hand speed and better anticipation, allowing them to react more quickly to opponents' shots

- Pressure handling: 5.0 players are better equipped to handle the increased pressure and pace of high-level play, maintaining their performance in challenging situations

- Overall court coverage and athleticism: 5.0 players typically display superior court coverage and athleticism, allowing them to reach and return more difficult shot

These differences collectively contribute to the higher level of play and competitive edge that 5.0 players have over 4.5 players.

Drills to reach the 5.0 level

Here are some key drills and focus areas:

- Backhand Reset Drill: Practice backhand resets consistently, as this is considered a crucial shot for advancing to the 5.0 level. Focus on soft grip and proper technique

- Reset and Counter Drill: Mix up resets with counters. Practice 2-3 resets in a row, then counter on the third attack. This helps develop variation in shot selection and improves offensive capabilities

- Hot Hands Drill: Stand at the kitchen line while a partner feeds hard pace balls from the baseline, varying left to right. This improves hand speed, reaction time, and volley skills. Start slow and gradually increase pace

- Hands Battle Drill: Stand 6-12 inches inside the kitchen line with a partner and trade volleys at about 75% speed. This builds hand speed and improves your ability to handle fast exchanges at the net

- Serve Variety Drill: Practice serving both deep and short, varying from left to right sides. This improves your ability to mix up serves and keep opponents off balance

- Drive and Drop Alternate Shots Drill: From the baseline, alternate between drive shots and drop shots while your partner feeds balls from the kitchen line. Aim for 10-20 consecutive successful shots. This improves shot selection and execution of both aggressive and soft shots

- Dinking Precision Drill: Focus on varying the depth, height, and speed of dinks. Practice creating "dead" dinks that are difficult for opponents to attack

- Third and Fourth Shot Execution Drill: Work on perfecting third shot drops and drives, as well as fourth shot strategies like angled backhand blocks to the opponent's feet

- Offensive Dinking Drill: Practice hitting offensive dinks past the kitchen line to put pressure on opponents

Reaching the 5.0 level also requires improvements in strategy, consistency, and mental game, not just technical skills. Incorporate these drills into your practice routine while also focusing on overall game improvement and tournament play experience.

Comparison of a 5.0 to a 5.5 pickleball player

The key differences between a 5.0 and a 5.5+ level pickleball player:

- Consistency and Precision:

- 5.5+ players have near-perfect consistency and precision in all aspects of their game.

- 5.0 players are highly consistent but may still make occasional errors under pressure.

- Tournament Performance:

- 5.5+ players consistently win or place highly in major tournaments. They have an extensive tournament win streak

- 5.0 players can compete at high levels but may not consistently win against top professionals.

- Skill Mastery:

- 5.5+ players have mastered every skill on the 5.0 skill assessment sheet and improved upon it

- 5.0 players have excellent skills but may still have room for improvement in some areas.

- Level of Excellence:

- 5.5+ players are considered "top caliber" by USA Pickleball and play at the highest level of excellence in both casual and tournament play

- 5.0 players are excellent but may not be at the absolute top level of the sport.

- Competitive Standing:

- There may be very few players who can go toe-to-toe with 5.5+ players

- 5.0 players are regionally some of the best players but may not be at the professional level

- Professional Status:

- Many 5.5+ players are likely to be professional or semi-professional players.

- 5.0 players, while extremely skilled, may not necessarily be playing at a professional level.

- Strategic Thinking:

- 5.5+ players have an extremely advanced understanding of strategy and can adapt their game plan instantly.

- 5.0 players have very good strategic skills but may not adapt as quickly or effectively as top professionals.

In essence, the jump from 5.0 to 5.5+ represents the difference between very skilled amateur players and top professional competitors. The 5.5+ rating is reserved for the elite players in the sport who consistently perform at the highest levels of competition.

www.ingramcontent.com/pod-product-compliance
Lightning Source LLC
Chambersburg PA
CBHW070136080526
44586CB00015B/1718